a full-length comedy

M*A*S*H

by

TIM KELLY

dramatized from the book

by RICHARD HOOKER

THE DRAMATIC PUBLISHING COMPANY

M*A*S*H
A Comedy in Two Acts
For Fifteen Men and Fifteen Women
(much smaller with doubling)

CHARACTERS
(in order of appearance)

GENERAL HAMILTON HARTINGTON HAMMOND

PVT. BOONE

LT. COLONEL HENRY BRAYMORE BLAKE

CAPTAIN BRIDGET McCARTHY

LT. JANICE FURY

SERGEANT DEVINE

LT. LOUISE KIMBLE

CAPTAIN FRANK BURNS

FATHER JOHN PATRICK MULCAHY

CAPTAIN WALTER WALDOWSKI (WALT)

CAPTAIN JOHN McINTYRE (TRAPPER JOHN)

CAPTAIN JOHN BLACK (UGLY)

CORPORAL "RADAR" REILLY

CAPTAIN BENJAMIN FRANKLIN PIERCE (HAWKEYE)

CAPTAIN AUGUSTUS BEDFORD FORREST (DUKE)

HO-JON

PVT. LOPEZ

KOREAN WOMAN #1

KOREAN WOMAN #2

LT. NANCY PHILLIPS

MAJOR MARGARET HOULIHAN

CONGRESSWOMAN GOLDFARB

DEAN MERCY LODGE

MISS RANDAZZLE

MITZI, FRITZI and AGNES

LT. CONNIE LIEBOWITZ

CAPTAIN OLIVER WENDELL JONES
(SPEARCHUCKER)

MAJOR RUTH HASKELL

G.I.'s, Koreans, Medical Personnel

PLACE: Compound of the 4077th Mobile
Army Surgical Hospital, Korea.

TIME: A period of many months during
the Korean Conflict.

ACT ONE
Scene One

In the darkened theatre we hear the menacing sound
   of artillery fire. It goes on for a few seconds,
   until --

LIGHTS COME UP on the office of General Hamilton
   Hartington Hammond, south of the city of Seoul.
   The office is nothing more than a small table or
   desk placed in front of the curtain, DR, on which
   are telephone, papers, etc.

   The office of Lt. -Colonel Henry Braymore Blake,
   commanding officer of MASH, is DL, also with
   a desk telephone, papers, etc.

   GENERAL HAMMOND, in full uniform, sits behind his desk holding the telephone receiver im-
   patiently. PVT. BOONE, Colonel Blake's clerk,
   holds the other receiver nervously, looking off L.)

GENERAL HAMMOND. . . . still there? . . . hello
   . . . ? (Shakes receiver.) What a lousy connec-
   tion. (Barks into mouthpiece.) Anybody out
   there!
BOONE (frightened). Yes, yes, General Hammond,
   sir. I'm here.
GENERAL HAMMOND. I don't want to talk to a private! I want to talk to a colonel. Colonel Blake!
   (BOONE almost drops the receiver.)

BOONE. Yes, sir, General Hammond, sir. He'll
    be here in a moment, sir.
GENERAL HAMMOND. He'd better be!

(COLONEL BLAKE, disheveled, ENTERS from DL.
    He's been interrupted while taking a shower. He
    wears long johns with his colonel's wings pinned
    on the shoulders. His feet are stuck into heavy,
    unlaced combat boots. He wears a cap with
    earflaps and dark sunglasses. There's a towel
    around his neck.)

COLONEL BLAKE. I wait all week for this call and
    it has to come when I'm in the shower.
BOONE. General's on a tear, Colonel Blake.
COLONEL BLAKE. Boone, you get out of here and
    get me some coffee. (BOONE dashes off, DL.)
    Strong coffee! Last cup you got me wouldn't
    even stain my shirt.
GENERAL HAMMOND (confused by the sounds com-
    ing through the receiver). Stain your shirt?
    (Shakes receiver again.) What is this? (Barks.)
    Henry, that you? Henry!
COLONEL BLAKE (on the mouthpiece). Now, listen,
    General. I gotta have two more men.
GENERAL HAMMOND. What do you think you're
    running up there? Walter Reed Army Hospital?
COLONEL BLAKE. Listen to me----
GENERAL HAMMOND. Take it easy, Henry.
COLONEL BLAKE. Don't Henry me. And I won't
    take it easy. If I don't get two new surgeons on
    my MASH team pronto----
GENERAL HAMMOND (cutting in again). All right!
    All right! So I'll send you the two best men I
    have. Satisfied?
COLONIAL BLAKE. They'd better be good, or I'll----
GENERAL HAMMOND. I said they'll be the two

best men I've got!

COLONEL BLAKE. Good! And get 'em here quick.
(COLONEL BLAKE slams down his receiver,
EXITS DL. GENERAL HAMMOND hangs up the
telephone.)

GENERAL HAMMOND. I'll get 'em there quick,
Henry. And, brother, are you in for a surprise!
(He stands, EXITS DR as the LIGHTS FADE.)

ACT ONE
Scene Two

THE CURTAIN OPENS on the MASH compound. [For
detailed description and stage chart, see Production Notes, pages 111-113.]

NOTE: All transitions from one scene to another
are done so the effect is of one picture blending
into another. There is always something happening onstage. [See Production Notes page 114.]

AT RISE OF CURTAIN: The MASH compound is alive.

In the nurses' tent, CAPTAIN BRIDGET
McCARTHY, an efficient and capable personality,
is seated on her foot locker, arranging her hair
into a tight bun. LT. JANICE FURY, young and
attractive, is exercising -- kneebends, twists,
et al.

In the mess tent, the cook, SERGEANT DEVINE,

is pouring coffee into some cups set out on the counter. A nurse, LT. KIMBLE, and CAPTAIN FRANK BURNS, a boorish stickler for proce- dure and the rule book, are seated at the down- stage table. A chaplain, FATHER JOHN PATRICK MULCAHY, sits at the second table reading a newspaper.

NURSES, DOCTORS, MILITARY PERSONNEL and KOREAN WORKERS are seen in Avenues "A," "B," and "C," coming and going.

NOTE: From time to time during the compound scenes, the director may want to have cast mem- bers make stage crosses to suggest the pulse of MASH life. Unless there is a specific reason for a particular character to make an appear- ance in some "Avenue" area, it is not indica- ted in the script, but it is a good idea to keep in mind the importance of optional stage activity. [See Production Notes, page 114 .]

The main focus is on "The Swamp." A foot locker has been pulled out and it serves as a card table. Three doctors are grouped around it playing poker. They are: CAPTAIN WALTER "WALT" WALDOWSKI, CAPTAIN JOHN McINTYRE, who goes by the name of "TRAPPER JOHN," and CAPTAIN "UGLY" JOHN BLACK, who, in typical MASH insanity, is called "UGLY" because he's actually quite good-looking. A fourth man, CORPORAL "RADAR" REILLY, is down on his hands and knees, his ear pressed to the floor of the tent.)

WALT. Anything yet?
RADAR. I can't hear anything if you're going to

keep asking me if I hear anything. (Afterthought.)
Sir.

TRAPPER. Radar, it's a good thing you've got special gifts. Otherwise, I'd boot you out of this
tent. You don't show proper respect for the
officer class.

RADAR. Wait, wait. I hear something now.

UGLY. What?

RADAR. Quiet.

TRAPPER and WALT (to UGLY). Quiet!

(In the mess tent, SERGEANT DEVINE brings coffee
to the downstage table. [See Production Notes
for suggestion on handling such shifts of action.])

DEVINE. Here we go.

LOUISE. Thanks, Sergeant.

BURNS (taking cup). You're wearing dirty fatigues,
Sergeant Devine. Merely because we're close
to the front lines is no reason to assume a
slovenly attitude.

DEVINE. Uh-huh.

BURNS. Uh-huh? Uh-huh what?

DEVINE. Uh-huh to what you said. (Then:) Sir.

BURNS. Don't get discourteous with me, Sergeant
Devine. I'll have you up before Colonel Blake.

DEVINE (taking out some travel folder). I was wondering, sir, if you'd care to purchase the band-
aid concession at Yankee Stadium?

BURNS. Nonsense.

DEVINE. I could let you have it cheap.

BURNS. You must take me for a fool. (Smugly.)
Besides, I happen to know you sold that concession to Major Hobson only last month. (On
this, FATHER MULCAHY looks up wide-eyed.
DEVINE shrugs, returns to his duties.)

(In the nurses' tent, JANICE has quit exercising.)

JANICE (exhausted). You'd think working in a mo-
bile Army unit would keep you in trim.
BRIDGET. I don't worry about it. I let it spread.
JANICE. If the kids I went to school with could see
me now. They didn't think I was good for much
except looking helpless.
BRIDGET. You do fine.
JANICE. When the artillery starts, I go weak in
the knees.
BRIDGET. Happens to all of us.
JANICE. Sometimes when I'm at the operating table
and those cases keep coming on day and night,
I get the feeling I'm going to faint.
BRIDGET. I wouldn't advise it. Most of the doc-
tors here are nice, but they're all a little crazy.
If a nurse faints in surgery they either use her
for a blood donor, or take bets on how long she'll
stay under. MASH is no place for a lady,
Lieutenant Fury. Remember that and you'll survive.
Come on, we've got the next shift. (BRIDGET
and JANICE EXIT their tent, going UR.)

(In "The Swamp," RADAR is convinced he's
on to something.)

RADAR. Yup. That's what it sounds like to me.
Helicopters. (The others tense.)
UGLY. How many?
RADAR (pressing ear to floor). More than six . . .
no, more than eight . . . nine. More, even!

(CAPTAINS BENJAMIN FRANKLIN PIERCE,
"HAWKEYE," and AUGUSTUS BEDFORD
FORREST, "DUKE," two young surgeons, have

ENTERED "Avenue C" from UL behind the mess
tent. They carry duffel bags and are dressed
sloppily. They look around, casing the compound.
DUKE points to "The Swamp." They cross to it.
Dialogue plays through.)

TRAPPER. Must have been that assault on Moonflower
Hill.

UGLY. I knew it would be a mean one.

WALT. Takes care of our poker game for the next
seventy-two hours. (HAWKEYE and DUKE are
standing at the stage left entrance to "The
Swamp.")

HAWKEYE. This the tent they call "The Swamp"?
(All look up to see the new arrivals. RADAR
goes back to his peculiar listening.)

(During the following scene, FATHER MULCAHY
will EXIT the mess tent and, in due time, so will
LOUISE. Later, SERGEANT DEVINE will leave
via exit flap in the rear of his "dining" emporium,
leaving only CAPTAIN BURNS.)

UGLY. Tent number six of the double natural: 4077th
Mobile Army Surgical Hospital.

TRAPPER. Astride the 38th Parallel.

WALT (like a travel agent). In lovely, romantic
South Korea.

RADAR (flat). Otherwise known as "The Swamp."

UGLY. And who might you gents be? (The two new
arrivals move into the tent.)

HAWKEYE. I'm Captain Benjamin Franklin Pierce.

WALT. That's a real name?

HAWKEYE. My friends call me Hawkeye. (Turns to
his buddy.) And this is Captain Augustus Bedford
Forrest, alias "Duke."

DUKE (with a feeble salute). Hiya.

ALL. Hiya.

TRAPPER. Did I hear right? Hawkeye?

HAWKEYE. Only book my old man ever read was
    "The Last of The Mohicans."

TRAPPER (excited). Your old man used to sell
    lobsters?

HAWKEYE. Still does. Nothing under a pound and
    a half, though.

TRAPPER. From Crabapple Cove, Maine?

HAWKEYE. Bull's-eye!

TRAPPER (flinging off his fatigue hat). Hawkeye,
    don't you remember me? Pride of Dartmouth
    College? McIntyre. John McIntyre. "Trapper
    John" McIntyre. (The name "Trapper John"
    rings the bell.)

HAWKEYE (throwing his arms wide). Trapper John!
    I'll be a speckled seagull! (TRAPPER JOHN and
    HAWKEYE embrace like long-lost brothers,
    dance around the tent like lunatic grizzly bears.)

TRAPPER. I knew there couldn't be two Hawkeyes
    in this cockeyed world!

HAWKEYE. Trapper John, you ole trapper, you!

TRAPPER. Lobster man!

UGLY (shaking hands with DUKE). I'm John Black.
    Everyone calls me Ugly. They call me Ugly
    because I'm good-looking. Understand?

DUKE. If you say so, Captain.

UGLY (introductions). This is Walt Waldowski. If
    you want to know where the real action is, it's
    in his tent.

WALT (shaking hands). The Painless Polish Poker
    Parlor and Dental Clinic. You guys get any
    trouble with your tusks, I'm the man to see.
    On Wednesdays and Fridays I run bingo games.
    Helps relieve the tension.

RADAR. Quiet!

WALT, TRAPPER and UGLY. Quiet! (HAWKEYE

and DUKE react, startled. A deadly hush falls
over the tent. Only now do the newcomers
notice RADAR with his ear to the floor. They
exchange a bewildered look.)

HAWKEYE. We don't mean to horn in, but----

ALL. Sssssshhhh. (HAWKEYE and DUKE can't
figure this one out and don't try.)

RADAR (getting up). Gonna be a busy night. Yes,
sir, a busy night. (He EXITS toward stage R,
into "Avenue A" and off.)

HAWKEYE. Somebody digging under the tent?

TRAPPER. No. That was Radar Reilly.

WALT. He's got the gift.

DUKE. Uh--what gift?

UGLY. He can anticipate what you're gonna say
before you say it. And he's got super-sensitive
ears. Why, Radar can hear things no other
mortal can. This tent is his best station for
receiving.

TRAPPER. We knew two new guys were coming
last week.

UGLY. Radar monitored the call from General
Hammond. (HAWKEYE and DUKE are impressed.)

HAWKEYE. Sounds like a good man to know. Where
do we bunk?

TRAPPER. In here with me. (Sour.) And Burns.

UGLY. I'll get Ho-Jon to unpack your duffels. (UGLY
moves to stage right entrance of "The Swamp.")

TRAPPER. You guys get the middle cots. (HAWKEYE
and DUKE toss their duffels on the middle cots.)

UGLY (yelling into "Avenue A"). Ho-Jon!

HAWKEYE (sitting on cot). Who's Burns?

WALT. Captain Frank Burns. And he'll never let
you forget it.

TRAPPER. Regular army. Goes watery in the eyes
when they play taps.

UGLY. Does surgery by the numbers. (Yells again.)

Ho-Jon!
DUKE (looking around). So "The Swamp" is home.
HAWKEYE. Better believe it.

(HO-JON, a small seventeen-year-old Korean, comes
    running into the compound from UR, behind the
    nurses' tent, and into "Avenue A.")

WALT (to HAWKEYE). Stay out of Burns' way. He
    can mean trouble. (HO-JON, energetic and
    anxious to please, is now standing outside "The
    Swamp." He wears fatigues, and like all
    Koreans he has the habit of putting an "S" sound
    on the end of some of his words.)
HO-JON. Here I am, sir, Captain.
UGLY. What took you so long? Two new butcher
    boys. Hop to it, Ho-Jon.
HO-JON. Yes, sir, Captain. Next time I'll run
    faster. (HO-JON enters tent. DUKE is unpack-
    ing his duffel.)
TRAPPER. Couple of live ones for you, Ho-Jon.
    (To HAWKEYE and DUKE) Best houseboy in
    the camp. Sews on buttons faster than the speed
    of lightning. If Ho-Jon can't find you what you
    want, it ain't available in the Republic of South
    Korea.
HO-JON (slight Oriental bow). I am very honored,
    gentlemen, sirs. (HAWKEYE and DUKE
    return the bow.)
DUKE. Same here.
HAWKEYE. Gotcha.
TRAPPER. Do you know who these esteemed
    doctors happen to be? (HO-JON is all smiles,
    thinking he's about to deliver a high compliment.)
    Oh, yes, sir. Two new butcher boys.
    (HAWKEYE and DUKE aren't exactly
    overwhelmed by the "flattery.")

Back to trapper

DUKE. They learn fast.

HO-JON (referring to DUKE'S unpacking). Oh, no,
      sir. My job. (Always smiling, he crosses
      quickly to the cot and takes the duffel from DUKE,
      begins to unpack it.)

      (During HO-JON'S introduction, BURNS gets up
      from the table in the mess tent, exits into
      "Avenue C" and moves to "The Swamp.")

WALT (the cards). You guys in?

DUKE. I'm game.

HAWKEYE. You're telling me.

DUKE. So I'll shower later. (DUKE, HAWKEYE,
      WALT, UGLY and TRAPPER JOHN group around
      the foot locker serving as table. BURNS enters
      "The Swamp" from L, frowns.)

BURNS. Captain Waldowski, why don't you play
      cards in your own tent?

WALT. Last night's rain washed out the floor.

TRAPPER. I asked him to play cards in this tent.

BURNS. It's also my tent and I wasn't consulted. In
      any case, I don't approve of frivolity in the com-
      pound. (Insufferably.) War is a very serious
      business. (All stare at BURNS. He really is a
      pompous ass. HAWKEYE belches. HO-JON
      suppresses a laugh.)

TRAPPER. Come off it, Burns.

BURNS. Captain, if you please.

TRAPPER. Well, I don't please. (Introductions.)
      This is Captain Forrest.

DUKE (a wave of the hand). Hi.

TRAPPER. Captain Pierce. (BURNS extends a hand.
      HAWKEYE prefers to belch a second time, which
      is his way of evaluating BURNS. This time
      HO-JON laughs out loud.)

BURNS (turning, angry). What are you laughing at?

(HO-JON , embarrassed, lowers his head.
What are you doing in here, anyway? (To others.)
Can't trust any of them. They're all thieves.
(HO -JON is shaken by the insult and terribly
hurt. He runs out of the tent R and off.)

WALT. Why did you have to say something like
    that?

BURNS. It's true.

WALT. It's not true and you know it. Don't take
    out your frustrations on Ho-Jon. He doesn't
    deserve them.

BURNS. He'll get over his hurt.

TRAPPER. You know, Burns, Koreans have feel-
    ings, too. That may come as a surprise to you.

BURNS. We have more important things to worry
    about. (To HAWKEYE.) I'm in charge of the
    first surgical shift. I imagine one of you two
    will take over the second.

(COLONEL BLAKE has ENTERED from DL and
    crosses to the left entrance of "The Swamp."
    PVT. BOONE is with him, holding a clipboard
    with papers.)

BLAKE (entering the tent, surveying the scene).
    Don't anybody yell attention on my account.

TRAPPER. Okay, Henry, we won't.

BLAKE. Pierce and Forrest. Where are they?
    (HAWKEYE and DUKE raise their hands
    like students in a classroom.)

HAWKEYE and DUKE. Here, teacher.

BLAKE. Wise guys, huh. That's all I need. Let
    me see your orders. (They fish out their orders
    and pass them to BLAKE.) 'Bout time you got
    here. I've been expecting you for two days.

DUKE. Jeep trouble.

BLAKE. Don't hand me any baloney about jeep

trouble. You were A.W.O.L. Living it up in
Seoul. I've heard plenty about you two. (Hands
orders to BOONE.) File this garbage under garbage.

BOONE (taking orders). Yes, sir.

BLAKE. You guys look like a pair of weirdos to me.
Maybe it's General Hammond's way of getting
even for all the static I've been giving him, but
if you work out well I'll hold still for a lot, and
if you don't I'll nail your tails to the tent flap.

DUKE (to HAWKEYE). Nice friendly sort.

BURNS. Colonel, sir. (BLAKE plainly doesn't think
too much of BURNS.)

BLAKE. What do you want?

BURNS. About the card playing that goes on twenty-
four hours a day. (BLAKE turns and EXITS L,
trailed by BOONE.)

BLAKE. Boone, file the Captain's complaint under
"J."

BOONE. "J, " sir?

BLAKE. "J" for junk. (BLAKE and BOONE EXIT
UL behind the mess tent. BURNS is incensed.)

BURNS. I don't see why the Colonel behaves like
that. My protest was in the best interest of the
unit's efficiency. You can't play cards and
checkers and chess all night and be alert in the
morning.

TRAPPER. Simmer down, Burns. You're heading
for a Section Eight.

WALT. 'Sides, there aren't going to be any games
for quite a spell.

BURNS. Why do you say that?

UGLY. Radar Reilly heard helicopters.

BURNS. That's nonsense. Believing Corporal
Reilly can hear and predict an alert. If there's
going to be a run of casualties we'll be notified
in advance through official channels. The army

way.   There won't be an emergency for several
days.

(On cue, a SIREN wails through the compound. Everyone jumps to his feet.)

HAWKEYE. Mighty short days, Captain Burns.

(The compound throbs with activity. NURSES,
KOREANS,MILITARY PERSONNEL hurry into the
"avenues" prepared for the worst. Some carry
medical cartons, plasma, blankets, et al.
LOUISE runs into the nurses' tent and grabs
her helmet liner, puts it on, runs out. The
"Swampmen" dash out of the tent R and L, leaving an angry CAPTAIN BURNS in their wake.
The SIREN continues to wail.)

Off
Right

(The LIGHTS FADE TO BLACKNESS and a
TRAVELLER CURTAIN cuts across the stage.
[See Production Notes on use of traveller
curtain.])

ACT ONE
Scene Three

(The alert siren continues to wail in the darkness . . .
    until COLONEL BLAKE'S voice comes over via
    loudspeaker.)

COLONEL BLAKE. Attention . . . attention . . .
    it's a big one. They hit Moonflower Hill.
    Casualties will be rolling in hot and heavy, day and
    night. You're gonna have your hands full.
    Twelve hour shifts. Full alert. All personnel
    report to usual stations--and that includes those
    two weirdos Pierce and Forrest. I'm gonna be
    watching you guys.

(CHARACTERS for Scene Three have ENTERED in
    the darkness. We hear the distant sound of
    artillery fire from time to time. Lights do not
    dim up. Seconds pass and one after another,
    flashlights snap on.)

DEVINE (flashlight on). What am I doing out here?
    I'm not a lighthouse, I'm a chef.
PVT. LOPEZ (flashlight on).   You're a lighthouse
    now. Keep the beam going and direct them
    whirlybirds in this direction.
RADAR (flashlight on). Two of 'em have already
    cracked up and one of 'em landed in the middle
    of the river.

KOREAN WOMAN #1 (flashlight on). All the doctors
     and nurses work like crazy people.
PVT. LOPEZ. They are crazy people. MASH isn't
     a hospital. It's a portable funny farm.
KOREAN WOMAN #2 (flashlight on). Buddha will
     help all the wounded. Trust Buddha. Buddha
     knows best.
PVT. LOPEZ. I hope Buddha knows how to land a
     night 'copter.
KOREAN WOMAN #1. Sky in the north is on fire.
     (Soft purring sound of approaching helicopters.)
DEVINE. As far as I'm concerned the fire can stay
     in the north.
RADAR. I hear 'em.
PVT. LOPEZ. Wave 'em southeast, otherwise
     they'll hit the mud. (PVT. LOPEZ waves his
     light as do the others. A few more flashlights
     snap on and the beams hit the roof of the theatre,
     making eerie crisscrosses. All motion the un-
     seen 'copters R. Sound of helicopters grows
     louder and louder as the actors move off DR. They
     yell into the darkness even though the pilots
     can't possibly hear them.)
ALL (ad libs).
          Over here!
          Hey, up there!
          Yahoo!
          This way!
          Down here!
          This way, this way!
          Etc.

(ALL move off DR. Sound of the helicopters is al-
     most deafening. It begins to fade -- until all is
     quiet. Slowly, a WARM LIGHT DIMS UP on the
     curtain to indicate that time of morning around
     dawn.)

(From behind the curtain comes the song of a
Korean softly singing some Oriental lullaby.
Exhausted MASH PERSONNEL saunter in, in
front of the curtain, from off DL. A couple
still have on their operating smocks. Among
the weary procession we discover those who
will speak.)

LOUISE. I wonder what it feels like to sleep.
WALT. I wouldn't know, but my hands will be wir-
    ing cracked jaws in my dreams. (They EXIT
    DR.)
FATHER MULCAHY. I don't think I'd like to see
    another night like that in some time.
UGLY (yawning). Never would be to soon for me.
    (They EXIT DR.)
BRIDGET. I'd have breakfast, only I don't think I
    could stay awake long enough to chew anything.

(HO-JON ENTERS from DL. Unlike the others, he's
    energetic. He carries fresh linen in his arms
    and there's a happy smile on his young face.)

HO-JON (brightly). New day, new work, new pro-
    mise. Just like in America.
BRIDGET (yawning loudly). They'll appreciate that
    in "The Swamp," Ho-Jon. They like spirits.
    (HO-JON moves along quickly in contrast to the
    slow gait of the others, EXITS DR.)

ACT ONE
Scene Four

THE TRAVELLER CURTAIN OPENS, revealing
    HAWKEYE and DUKE stretched out on their cots
    asleep, snoring softly.

    In time, SERGEANT DEVINE will appear from
    behind the flap in the rear of the mess tent and
    set about his chores.

    In the nurses' tent, JANICE is trying to comfort
    a sobbing friend, LT. NANCY PHILLIPS, who
    sits on the edge of the downstage cot.)

JANICE.   Look, Nancy, it could happen to anyone.
NANCY.   It didn't happen to anyone. It happened to
    me. Got a handkerchief--anything? (JANICE
    pulls a handkerchief from some pocket.)
JANICE.   Here.
NANCY (taking it, wiping her nose). I'm going to ask
    for a transfer.
JANICE.   That's foolish.
NANCY.   Nothing like this has ever happened to me
    before. I've never been spoken to like that by
    any doctor. He's getting meaner all the time.

(HO-JON ENTERS compound from UR, enters

"Avenue A" and goes into "The Swamp," R.)

JANICE. You're an excellent nurse and you didn't
    foul up.

(HO-JON tiptoes to the sleeping DUKE and HAWKEYE.
    He sees that DUKE has fallen asleep without a
    blanket, pulls one up from the foot of the cot and
    covers him after putting down his armful of
    clean linen. When this is done, he moves out
    left and crosses over and into mess tent.)

NANCY. I feel like such a fool, breaking down like
    this.
JANICE. You've been up eighteen hours.

(BRIDGET ENTERS the tent UR, sees that some-
    thing is wrong.)

BRIDGET. You two don't exactly look joyous.
NANCY. You haven't heard about it?
BRIDGET. I'm too tired for guessing games.
    Heard about what?
NANCY. Captain Burns left me in charge of the re-
    covery tent. One of the men was dead as soon
    as they carried him in. I brought up a suction
    machine.
JANICE (to BRIDGET).   It wouldn't have helped.
NANCY. I had to do something, to try. Anyway, the
    suction machine wasn't functioning.
JANICE. Neither was the patient.
NANCY . Captain Burns came in while I was try-
    ing to work the machine and right in front of
    everyone he yelled out, "Lieutenant Phillips,
    you've killed my patient."
BRIDGET. Sounds like him all right. What a
    stinking thing to say.
NANCY. I think it would be better if I transferred.

BRIDGET. I don't. And I'm in charge here until
    headquarters sends a new chief nurse. Get
    some sleep. We'll talk about it when you're
    feeling more like yourself.
JANICE. Sure. That's all you need. Sleep. You're
    dog-tired, (Too weary to argue, NANCY falls
    back on her cot. BRIDGET indicates that she
    and JANICE ought to leave her alone. They
    EXIT the tent toward DR and off.)

(In the mess tent, HO-JON has gotten two cups of
    coffee from DEVINE and takes them back into
    "The Swamp." He sets them down on the floor
    beside the cots of HAWKEYE and DUKE.
    CAPTAIN BURNS has ENTERED the compound
    from UR behind the nurses' tent and crossed to
    the right entrance of "The Swamp," enters,
    spots HO-JON.)

BURNS. What are you in here for now?
HO-JON(putting his finger to his lips). Sssh. They
    sleep. Very tired.
BURNS. What do you think I am--alive and kicking?
    (Grabs HO-JON by the arm.) Were you
    trying to steal something?
HO-JON. Oh, no, sir. Captain Burns.
HAWKEYE (waking, annoyed). Hey, Burns, hold it
    down, will you?
HO-JON. Captain Pierce, sir. I didn't steal any-
    thing.
BURNS (to HO-JON). Get out of my tent. I want
    to sleep.
HAWKEYE (sitting up). Your tent?
BURNS. Mine as much as yours.
DUKE (now awake). Burns, why don't you go drown
    yourself in a rice paddy?
BURNS. Don't you talk that way to me. I'm regular

army and I have seniority.

HAWKEYE. I'll buy you a medal. (Stands.) Let's
    get something straight, Burns. We don't like
    you. We don't like you for several reasons.
    For starters, you're the kind of dude who
    blames every mistake on someone else.

DUKE. Like the little scene with Lieutenant
    Phillips.

BURNS. She's incompetent.

DUKE. That soldier died because you're a lousy
    surgeon. You're a quack.

BURNS (incredulous). Quack? (Angry.) Quack!

HAWKEYE. Quack, quack yourself.

DUKE. That's the biggest thing we've got against
    you. We don't like quacks.

HAWKEYE. Also, you're a pest.

BURNS. I don't have to take this.

HAWKEYE. Then don't. (With that, HAWKEYE
    pushes BURNS, heels over, onto his cot.)

DUKE. Come on, Hawkeye. Let's get some cof-
    fee. There's a bad taste in my mouth. (HO-JON
    runs out of the tent R, into "Avenue A" and out
    DR. HAWKEYE and DUKE leave "The Swamp"
    and cross for the mess tent. Infuriated, BURNS
    sits up and yells after them.)

BURNS. I'm not a quack! (Then.) I'm a captain.

(During the preceding scene, BLAKE has ENTERED
    the mess tent and SERGEANT DEVINE has
    brought him a cup of coffee.

In "The Swamp, " unobtrusively, BURNS strips
    down, takes a pair of pajamas from his foot
    locker and puts them on over his underwear.
    He pulls some ear plugs from the top pocket
    and puts them in. Next, he climbs into bed and
    goes to sleep. All this stage business is

performed while the scene in the mess tent plays.

DEVINE leans on the counter reading some
magazine. HAWKEYE and DUKE enter the
mess tent.)

DUKE. Just the man we want to see (He and
    HAWKEYE move to the downstage table and sit
    with BLAKE.)
HAWKEYE. Gotta talk with you, Henry.
BLAKE. Well, I don't want to talk with you. And
    don't call me Henry.
HAWKEYE. Henry, we don't want to cause you
    any trouble.
DUKE.. But we strongly suspect that something
    that might embarrass this excellent organiza-
    tion could occur if you don't get that quack out
    of our tent.
BLAKE. Are you two weirdos, by any chance, speak-
    ing of Captain Burns.
HAWKEYE.   The same.
BLAKE. He stays.
DUKE. He goes.
BLAKE. I can't afford to lose him. Look, I know
    your records. You're two of the best battle
    surgeons in Korea. You're unorthodox, but
    you're good. Still, I need every man I can get.
    That includes Burns.
HAWKEYE. You don't need Burns. (DEVINE eaves-
    drops for a few seconds, then EXITS via the
    rear of the mess tent.)
DUKE. We appreciate your position, Henry.
BLAKE. I doubt that. Don't call me Henry.
HAWKEYE. And as long as we're here we're going
    to do the best job we can.
BLAKE. Don't you think I know that?
DUKE. When the work comes our way we will do

all in our power to promote the surgical
efficiency of the outfit because that's what we
hired on for.

BLAKE. I like the way you boys talk.

HAWKEYE. But you may have to put up with a few
things from us that haven't been routine around
here. A guy like Burns is more trouble than
he's worth. We can handle his work as well as
our own.

DUKE. Faster, too.

HAWKEYE. We're asking you to get rid of him.
Transfer him.

DUKE. Send him back to the States.

HAWKEYE. Anything. Savvy?

BLAKE. I savvy. (HAWKEYE and DUKE beam in
triumph.)

DUKE. Then you've made your decision?

BLAKE. I have. (Gulps a swallow of coffee, slams
down the cup.) Captain Burns stays right where
he is. (HAWKEYE and DUKE grimace.)

(The TRAVELLER CURTAIN closes.)

ACT ONE
Scene Five

JANICE ENTERS DR. UGLY, with a stethoscope
around his neck, ENTERS DL.)

JANICE. Been looking all over the compound for
you.
UGLY (smiling). Well, well, well. Lieutenant
Fury, queen of the bedpans.
JANICE (stopping, folding her arms). I don't know
what there is about military life that changes the
male animal into a careless brute. If the
nurses in MASH ever got a compliment from one
of you doctors we'd probably fold up and fly
away on the breeze. (Though their banter is
easy, it's plain to see that JANICE and UGLY
have eyes for each other.)
UGLY (beside her). That's what you'd have us
believe. Don't forget, Lieutenant, I've gazed
into your eyes over a thoracotomy, a hemorrhage
and a lung removal. Surely that proves my
admiration.
JANICE. A hemorrhage? You certainly know how
to put romance in a girl's heart.
UGLY. You and the Rock of Gibraltar are made of
the same stuff.
JANICE (frowning). Stone?
UGLY. Come on, Fury, don't go all feminine on me.
JANICE. Fat chance in this open-air boiler room.

UGLY. What's on your mind?

JANICE. Dance.

UGLY (looking around). I don't hear any music.

JANICE. There isn't any. Unless it's in my head.
You stick around the double natural long enough
and you're bound to hear things.

UGLY. Aha, cynicism and medicine. The ideal
combination.

JANICE. We're heads of the dance committee--
or have you forgotten?

UGLY (bowing). At your service.

JANICE. Nothing drastic. All I want you to do is
see that "the boys" behave themselves. Be nice
to "the girls." Act like----

UGLY. Gentlemen?

JANICE. Gentlemen? No, that would be too much
to expect. Merely ask them to act--"humanely."
Same as they would with homeless dogs and
backward children.

UGLY. Good as done--if you save me the first and
last dance.

JANICE. Why, Captain Ugly, I do believe that's a
compliment. (He guides her DR, EXITING.)

UGLY. You know what they say, Lieutenant Fury.

JANICE. Tell me.

UGLY. A day without an Ugly compliment is like
a day without sunshine.

JANICE. Sometimes, Captain, I think I'd rather
have the rain. (They are out.)

ACT ONE
Scene Six

CURTAIN OPENS. HO-JON is standing in "Avenue
B," in front of "The Swamp," lecturing some
of the Korean workers. They hunker or sit on
the ground. BRIDGET stands in "Avenue C,"
eavesdropping.)

HO-JON. . . . And in America when you are hungry,
you eat something called the French Fry and
the Overheated Dog.
KOREAN WOMAN #1 (nodding happily). Dog tastes good.
HO-JON. And everybody sleeps in a bed. (KOREANS
"oooh" and "aaah," impressed.) Also, everyone
can read and write. Everyone has shoes.
KOREAN WOMAN #1. No, not so. Not shoes.
HO-JON. Is so. Captain Hawkeye Pierce and
Captain Duke Forrest say it is so. (This seems to
placate the dissenters. More "oohs" and
"aaahs.") Also, is a great country with many
historical persons. Captain Hawkeye Pierce
has had me memorize them.
KOREAN WOMAN #1. Tell us who they are.
HO-JON (beaming). There is Mr. G. Washington,
Mr. Lincoln, Mr. J. Kennedy and the famous
Mr. Liberace. (More ooohs and aaahs.)

(KOREAN WOMAN #2 ENTERS from DR carrying
a suspicious-looking bundle in her arms.)

KOREAN WOMAN #2. Pssst. Ho-Jon. (HO-JON
    looks over, sees her, claps his hands.)
HO-JON. Go now. Tomorrow I show you how to
    walk like a cowboy from big Texas. (On this
    promise there is great delight. The "aaah" is
    enthusiastic. KOREANS get up, EXIT L and R.
    HO-JON crosses to WOMAN #2 and takes the
    bundle. She turns and EXITS DR. HO-JON
    crosses to "The Swamp," enters the tent. He
    goes to the foot locker of Captain Burns,
    kneels down and takes something from the
    bundle and places it in the locker.)

(From UR, behind the nurses' tent, and into "Avenue
    A," come CAPTAIN BURNS, COLONEL BLAKE,
    and a new arrival, MAJOR MARGARET
    HOULIHAN. She's tall, nice-looking. BRIDGET
    has entered the mess tent by now. No one's about
    so she gets herself a cup of tea and sits down.)

BLAKE. I'm very happy, Major Houlihan. We've
    been most anxious about our new Chief Nurse.
MARGARET. Thank you, Colonel. I'm here now.
    Rest easy. (To BURNS.) You handle one of the
    surgical shifts, Captain Burns?
BURNS. I do.
MARGARET. And the other? (Silence.) I asked
    about the second shift.
BLAKE. That's handled by Hawkeye.
MARGARET. Hawkeye?
BURNS. Captain Benjamin Pierce. He calls himself
    Hawkeye.
MARGARET. That's odd.
BURNS. So's he. (To BLAKE.) Actually, Colonel,
    I've been meaning to speak to you about Hawkeye,
    uh, I mean Captain Pierce. (BLAKE has no
    intention of getting involved.)

BLAKE . Yes, well, put it in writing. If I can be
     of any further help in getting you settled, Major
     Houlihan, don't hesitate to seek me out. That's
     what I'm here for.
MARGARET.   Thank you so much, Colonel. (BLAKE
     tosses a lax salute, EXITS DR.)
BURNS. I'm certain we'll work out well together,
     Major.
MARGARET. I hope so, Captain.
BURNS. I should warn you about Hawkeye.
MARGARET. You mean Captain Pierce?
BURNS. Yes, that's right. He and his sidekick,
     Captain Forrest, are not the most reliable types.
MARGARET . Oh?
BURNS. According to him I'm quack, quack.
MARGARET. Quack, quack?
BURNS (nodding his head). Quack, quack.
     (MARGARET is mystified.)
MARGARET. Are we talking about ducks?
BURNS. Absolutely no respect.
MARGARET. Me? Or the ducks?
BURNS. I mean Pierce and Forrest. (MARGARET
     is desperately trying to fathom what BURNS is
     talking about.)
MARGARET. They don't respect you. Is that what
     you're trying to say?
BURNS. Has nothing to do with me. They don't
     respect the military manual. Or anything else,
     for that matter. They're individuals and I'm
     positive you agree, as I do, that individualism
     and the army are not compatible.
MARGARET. For the most part, yes.
BURNS. Splendid. If you'll excuse me now I'll sink
     into "The Swamp." (HO-JON has been stand-
     ing close to the right entrance of "The Swamp."
     He overhears BURNS and quickly hides under
     one of the bunks. BURNS enters the tent.)

MARGARET. Swamp? (Calls after him.) Captain,
     are you feeling all right? A touch of the sun,
     perhaps? (MARGARET doesn't know quite what
     to make of BURNS. What's he talking about?
     Ducks? Swamps? She shrugs, crosses in
     front of the mess tent and EXITS.)

          (DEVINE ENTERS the mess tent.)

DEVINE. Hi, Captain.
BRIDGET. Where you been?
DEVINE. As president of the Brooklyn and Manhattan
     Marked-down Monument and Landmark Company,
     I have many affairs to attend to.
BRIDGET. One of these days you're going to meet
     a cookie who's a bit too smart for your con
     games and then it's the M.P.'s for you, my boy.
DEVINE. Tut, tut, Captain McCarthy, you're a pessimist.
BRIDGET. I get that way from eating in here.

     (In "The Swamp," BURNS has sat on his cot and
     begun to unlace his boots. However, there's
     something unpleasant in the air. He sniffs. He
     makes a face. He stands, continuing to sniff. He
     moves close to his foot locker and realizes the
     offending odor is within. He kneels down, opens the
     locker and reaches in--coming out with the carcass
     of a dead cat, which he holds up by the tail as if it
     were the vilest thing in the world.)

BURNS. Ugh! (He drops the cat into the locker,
     slams it shut, and dashes to the right entrance
     of "The Swamp" and stands facing "Avenue A,"
     bellowing out his indignation.) I'll get you for
     this, Hawkeye! You and Forrest. You're in
     this together! This time you've gone too far!

(KOREANS, NANCY, and BOONE crowd into "Ave-
     nue A" from UR and DR, attracted by the sound
     of the raving BURNS.)

     (Unseen by BURNS, HO-JON crawls out from
     under the cot, jumps to his feet, makes for the
     foot locker and retrieves the dead cat. Swiftly,
     he darts out left, into "Avenue C," and EXITS
     UL behind the mess tent.)

NANCY. What's wrong, Captain Burns?
BURNS (outraged). When I get my hands on you guys!
BOONE (to NANCY). Maybe I ought to get the Colonel.

(KOREANS are mumbling excitedly. FATHER
     MULCAHY appears from DR. BRIDGET and
     DEVINE, hearing the commotion, exit mess
     tent, cross down to left of "The Swamp," peer in.)

FATHER MULCAHY. What's all the hoopla?
BURNS. Come in. I'll show you. (BURNS stands
     aside to admit FATHER MULCAHY and NANCY.
     BOONE enters, too. KOREANS crowd around
     the right entrance to "The Swamp," fascinated.)
FATHER MULCAHY. Well? (BURNS marches to the
     foot locker, points.)
BURNS. Open that and tell me what you see. (FATHER
     MULCAHY looks to NANCY.)
NANCY. Better do it. (She holds up her hands in
     bewilderment. FATHER MULCAHY opens the
     foot locker.)
BURNS. What do you think of that?
FATHER MULCAHY (peering in). I think you need
     some new underwear and there's a button miss-
     ing on your Ike jacket.
BURNS (still fuming). No, no. The cat.
FATHER MULCAHY. What cat?

BURNS. What cat?

FATHER MULCAHY. That's what I just got through
    saying.

BURNS. I'm speaking of the cat in my foot locker.

NANCY. Cat in your foot locker? Did I hear you
    right?   ·

FATHER MULCAHY. Captain Burns, there is no
    cat in this foot locker.

BURNS (annoyed). Let me in there. (He pushes
    aside FATHER MULCAHY, dives into the foot
    locker, tossing out shirts, socks, pants, etc.
    No cat! He sits on the floor, exhausted.) Some-
    body stole my cat. (BOONE runs out of the
    tent right and EXITS DR.)

BOONE (as he runs). Colonel Blake! Colonel
    Blake! It's Section Eight time! (NANCY moves
    to BURNS, puts a comforting hand to his shoul-
    der.)

NANCY. You'll be all right.

FATHER MULCAHY. Battle fatigue? (NANCY
    gravely nods her head "yes.")

NANCY. Relax. We'll have you fit in no time.
    Don't worry about a thing.

BURNS (looking like a six-year-old-child). Somebody
    stole my cat. (He sticks his thumb in his mouth,
    unaware of his damaged image. NANCY and
    FATHER MULCAHY shake their heads sorrow-
    fully. BRIDGET and DEVINE sigh.)

(The TRAVELLER CURTAIN closes.)

ACT ONE

Scene Seven

JANICE, LOUISE, RADAR and others cross from
   DL to DR. In their arms are lanterns, a
   portable record player, some inflated balloons;
   decorations for the approaching dance. Over
   the loudspeaker, we can hear the voice of
   WALT.)

WALT. 'Tenshun -- your attention, please. This
   is friendly Ole Walt Waldowski here reminding
   all you kiddies out there in MASHland that tomorrow evening being Friday, Bingo will be
   conducted in the Painless Polish Poker Parlor
   and Dental Clinic as is the custom. Twenty-
   five cents a card, five for a dollar. Winners
   of previous jackpots are not eligible to win a-
   gain. Sorry about that. Please hold off on all
   dental emergencies -- if possible. Over and
   out.

(During the stage cross activity, Colonel Blake's
   desk and chair have been placed DL. BLAKE
   ENTERS and sits at desk.

   (HAWKEYE and DUKE have ENTERED DR and
   cross behind JANICE and the others. They exchange friendly "Hiya's" and walk on to Blake's

office. DUKE pantomimes a knock.)

BLAKE. Come in! (DUKE pantomimes opening
    the door and they enter.)
HAWKEYE. Wanted to see us, Henry?
BLAKE. I did, and don't call me Henry.(Shuffles
    through papers on his desk.) I've got some-
    thing here for you birds. (Tosses papers all
    over the top of his desk.) Boone! Get your
    pinhead in here!

(BOONE zooms in from DL.)

BOONE. Yes, sir, Colonel Blake, sir. I'm here.
BLAKE. Where's that commendation General
    Hammond sent up for Captains Pierce and
    Forrest?
BOONE. You told me to file it in the incinerator.
BLAKE. I did? Never mind. Get back to your
    duties.
BOONE (saluting). Yes, sir, Colonel Blake.
BLAKE. And don't trip on your way out.
BOONE. No, sir. Thank you, sir. (BOONE EXITS
    DL, tripping over his boots on the way out.)
DUKE. You might have given us the opportunity to
    see it, Henry.
BLAKE. Would only puff out your fat heads. He
    was very pleased with your work here. Re-
    covery rate is way up.
HAWKEYE (shaking hands with DUKE). Congratu-
    lations, Captain Forrest.
DUKE. Congratulations, Captain Pierce.
BLAKE. You guys are riding high. You're first-
    class chest cutters. But you know it. You
    ought to be more humble.
HAWKEYE. Why?
BLAKE! Give me time and I'll think up a good

answer. Anyway, you won that round with Burns.
I had to reassign him stateside after rest and
relaxation in Tokyo. You had to do it, didn't
you? You just had to have your own way.

DUKE. Come off it, Henry.

BLAKE. Don't call me, Henry. Burns was a jerk,
I admit, but he was needed and now we don't
have him and it's your fault.

DUKE. Even Major Houlihan said he was cracking
up.

BLAKE. Never mind what Major Houlihan said. I
know you two. I know what you're capable of
and I know you drove Captain Burns psycho.

HAWKEYE. Things will be much nicer without him.

BLAKE. I'll be the judge of that. Go on, get out.
And remember--don't try my patience too far.

DUKE. Thanks again for showing us the General's
commendation, Henry.

BLAKE (rising behind the desk, livid). Don't
call me Henry!

(HAWKEYE and DUKE walk to the pantomimed
open doorway and EXIT, moving C as the
TRAVELLER CURTAIN OPENS and BLAKE
EXITS DL.)

ACT ONE
Scene Eight

When the TRAVELLER CURTAIN has opened the
    desk and chair are struck. HAWKEYE and
    DUKE are standing in "Avenue B."

In the nurses' tent, NANCY is putting on a ci-
    vilian dress, somewhat out-of-date.

In "The Swamp," UGLY and RADAR are playing
    chess, using a foot locker for a table.

DEVINE is behind his counter in the mess tent
    and MARGARET and BRIDGET are eating from
    metal trays, seated at the downstage table.

A few members of cast pass from one area to
    another. HO-JON hurries in from DR holding
    a neatly pressed pair of fatigues. All smiles,
    he moves to HAWKEYE and DUKE.)

HO-JON. All washed and pressed real clean,
    Captain Hawkeye. I stay up all the night.
HAWKEYE. Ho-Jon, you're a wonder.
DUKE (taking out some paper scrip). Here you go,
    Ho-Jon, buy yourself something from the PX.
HO-JON. No, no, Captain Duke. Not money until
    payday. Maybe you let me borrow another

book about your America?

DUKE. Done.

HO-JON. Captains, will you have any more need for
dead cats? I can get very old dead cats very cheap.

HAWKEYE. No, Ho-Jon, at the moment we're out of
the dead cat market. "Operation Douse Burns"
was a complete success.

DUKE. Thanks to MASH teamwork.

HAWKEYE. Seen Major Houlihan around?

HO-JON. In the mess tent with Captain McCarthy.
(HO-JON moves to the right entrance of "The
Swamp," and hangs up the clean fatigues as if they
were evening clothes. When this is done, he watches
the chess game.)

(KOREAN WOMAN #1 has ENTERED the nurses' tent
and she begins to clean up with a broom. NANCY
models the dress and KOREAN WOMAN #1 is duly
impressed.

HAWKEYE and DUKE move to "Avenue C," cross
up to the mess tent and enter. Dialogue of
MARGARET and BRIDGET is spoken during the
preceding.)

BRIDGET. Captain Black is probably the best man for
cardiac massage.

MARGARET. Yes, I think you're right. Still, every
everything here is done rather----

BRIDGET. Sloppily?

MARGARET. I wouldn't say sloppily but I suppose,
in a way, that's what I mean.

BRIDGET. All we can do here is patch 'em up and send
them on to the real thing. A hospital with clean
sheets.

MARGARET. And cleaner doctors.

(HAWKEYE and DUKE enter the mess tent.
MARGARET looks up and sees them.)

MARGARET. Oh, Captain Pierce, I wonder if I
    might have a word with you?
BRIDGET. I'll be on my way.
HAWKEYE (moving down). No need to run on my account.
BRIDGET. Got things to do and, Hawkeye, that Korean
    kid in "The Swamp" thinks you and Duke are a com-
    bination between Old Glory and Moses.
HAWKEYE. Yeah, yeah.
BRIDGET (to MARGARET). None of these kids have
    had much of a life. Ho-Jon lost most of his
    family in the early bombings. (BRIDGET
    crosses to the counter and puts her tray on it,
    nods to DUKE, EXITS the tent and off UL.
    DEVINE pours DUKE a cup of coffee.)
MARGARET. Captain Pierce.
HAWKEYE. Call me Hawkeye.
MARGARET. I prefer to call you Captain Pierce.
    It's better form.
DUKE (sipping his coffee). Cheers.
MARGARET. I observed the night shift and I was
    not at all impressed with some of our nurses.
    How do you feel about the nursing situation here?
HAWKEYE. Major, this is a team effort. I'm
    responsible for my team. It consists of doctors,
    nurses and enlisted men. We've been working
    as a unit for months with little change in
    personnel. I'm satisfied with them. Any
    further questions?
MARGARET (standing). I wonder how anyone like you
    reaches such a position of responsibility in the
    Army Medical Corps.
DUKE. If we knew the answer to that we wouldn't
    be here.
MARGARET. Very well. It appears that we are

not going to get along. Nevertheless, I want
you to know that I will attempt to cooperate
with you in every possible way.

HAWKEYE. Cool it, Houlihan.

MARGARET. I beg your pardon?

HAWKEYE. You never begged for anything in your
life and you know it. You're breathing fire all
the time. That's a good way to get hot lips.
And indigestion.

MARGARET. You're rude. And crude.

HAWKEYE. Simmer down, Hot Lips.

MARGARET (offended). Don't you dare address me
in that fashion.

HAWKEYE. This is a battle zone, not a veterans'
hospital stateside.

MARGARET. I am well aware of that.

(NANCY exits nurses' tent and, in time, KOREAN
WOMAN #1 finishes up her work and EXITS,
too, DR.)

HAWKEYE. The important thing is to watch with an
eye to how many people work happily or
unhappily, and if they're unhappy--why? If
you clear up that, you clear up inefficiency.

MARGARET (trying to hold her temper). The nurses
working with you and Captain Forrest refer to
you as Hawkeye and to him as Duke.

DUKE. Our names.

MARGARET. Such familiarity is highly improper
and inconsistent with maximum efficiency in an
organization such as this.

DUKE. Major, obviously you're a female version
of the routine Regular Army clown.

MARGARET. How dare you! I am a lady and an
officer.

HAWKEYE. Yes, ma'am. Stay away from me

and my gang and we'll get along fine.
(HAWKEYE gets up and moves to exit with DUKE.
He turns.) See you around campus.
DUKE (not unfriendly). See you, Hot Lips. (They
    exit out of the mess tent and off DL. MARGARET
    is shattered. She doesn't know what to do and
    speaks to DEVINE out of desperation.)
MARGARET. They're certainly not officers.
    They're certainly not gentlemen. And it's a
    mystery to me how they ever got to be surgeons.
DEVINE. Uh-huh. 'Scuse me, ma'am, but would
    you be interested in purchasing half interest
    in the Starlight Casino in Moose Jaw, Canada?
    (Utterly defeated, MARGARET sits with a
    groan, slamming her clenched fists against her
    temples.)

(The TRAVELLER CURTAIN closes.)

ACT ONE
Scene Nine

Music is piped over the loudspeaker. Dance music--
    an "oldie but goodie." If possible, balloons
    drop from overhead, or some KOREANS ENTER
    DL and DR with lighted lanterns on long poles.
    Several couples are dancing.

    TRAPPER JOHN and NANCY ENTER L and begin
    to dance; WALT and LOUISE ENTER R, dance.
    BRIDGET is dancing with PVT. LOPEZ. A
    few of the nurses, like NANCY, have managed
    to dig up some civilian odds-and-ends. Most,
    however, have simply added some "festive"
    touch to their fatigues; Hawaiian shirts, flower
    leis, funny hats, etc. Music ends. Applause.
    FATHER MULCAHY ENTERS DR.)

FATHER MULCAHY. Coffee and sandwiches over
    this way in a few minutes. Compliments of
    Sergeant Devine. (Scattered applause on
    announcement.)
AD LIBS.
        Great.
        I'm hungry.
        Let's eat.

WALT. Shall we dine?

LOUISE (like a "hammy" actress). Delighted, sir.
(WALT and LOUISE cross DR, converse with
FATHER MULCAHY.)

(UGLY ENTERS from L, wearing dirty fatigues.
Sub rosa ad lib conversation.)

UGLY (moving C). Hey, what is this? I thought
we were going to have a party. Where's the
music? Where's the dancing? Where are the
girls? (JANICE, who had been talking with
some of the dancers, crosses to him.)

JANICE. I thought you were going to behave for
once.

UGLY. I'm behaving.

JANICE. You were supposed to help with the
decorations.

UGLY. I'm ready.

JANICE. Not now. And look at those fatigues.

UGLY. What's the matter with them?

JANICE. Try introducing them to soap and water.

UGLY. What for?

JANICE. For the ladies, the girls. Remember?

UGLY. What ladies? Nobody here but nurses.

BRIDGET (calling over). Ignore him, Janice. He's
only a doctor.

UGLY (clapping his hands for attention). Listen,
everybody, I've got a treat. (By now, most
of the cast should be on stage with the exception
of Radar, Blake, Margaret, Hammond, Hawkeye,
Duke, Ho-Jon, Devine, and characters we have
yet to meet. BOONE, FATHER MULCAHY,
WALT and LOUISE are R; NANCY, TRAPPER
JOHN, BRIDGET and LOPEZ are L; others,
as best fits the stage picture. Continuing like
an M.C.) We gentlemen of the double natural

know we sometimes treat you gals pretty rough.
(Applause, cheers from the nurses.) But to
show you that we love you, we concocted a little
entertainment for your pleasure and it will be
performed by those daring and talented
troubadours--Hawkeye Pierce and Duke Forrest!

(More applause. HAWKEYE and DUKE ENTER
through the center of the curtain in top hat and
carrying canes. There is a murmur of delight
from the onlookers. A spotlight, maybe. The
"entertainers" sing to the tune of: "If I Had
the Wings of an Angel.")

HAWKEYE and DUKE.
            Oh, if we had the wings of a Colonel
            We'd fly to the high Pyrenees,
            And open an open-air laundry
            Specializing in Blake's B.V.D.'s.
(Applause, laughter from onlookers. HAWKEYE
and DUKE work in a little soft shoe for the next
verses.)
            Oh, if we break a leg in the morning,
            Or, if we break an elbow at noon,
            We've got nurses to help us get better.
            But we won't want them under the moon.
(Catcalls, hoots from nurses. Scattered laughter
from the men.)
            Oh, Margaret's a lady from Erin,
            Yes, Houlihan's Irish colleen.
            Her face has a touch of the shamrock.
            Don't kiss her--your lips will turn green.

(COLONEL BLAKE has escorted MARGARET in DL,
and they have heard the last stanza in full. As
HAWKEYE and DUKE finish, they throw out
their arms and wonder why there is no applause.

Questioningly, their eyes wander DL, and they
see BLAKE and MARGARET giving them an icy
look. They grin like apes.)

HAWKEYE (feebly). Uh, hi, Henry.
DUKE (waving his fingers childishly). Hiya, Hot
    Lips. (Quickly.) Er, uh, Major.
BLAKE. I see Broadway's loss is MASH'S loss.
    (General laughter.)
JANICE (hoping to ease tension). Uh, uh, glad you
    could make it, Colonel Blake.
BLAKE. Wouldn't've missed it for anything.
FATHER MULCAHY (moving C). Come on, everyone
    find partners. Forget this is South Korea.
    Forget we're in a battle zone. Use your imagi-
    nation. You're back home. Pretend this is
    your high school graduation dance. Come on,
    Colonel, you lead it off. (Music begins again.
    BLAKE and MARGARET continue to give
    HAWKEYE and DUKE the evil eye, but they
    settle into the mood. BLAKE and MARGARET
    dance, rather stiffly. After a few moments,
    others begin to dance, too--WALT with LOUISE,
    TRAPPER JOHN and NANCY, BRIDGET and
    LOPEZ, etc. Others can change partners.
    There is some cutting in by the "stag line."

At this point it would be effective to have one of
the nurses or G.I.'s who has a good voice sing
along for the dancing. The effect we're striving
for is one that suggests another period in the
lives of the MASH personnel, a younger time, a
gentler time.

HAWKEYE and DUKE look for partners, but the
nurses all have partners. They shrug, begin to dance
with each other. Music is cut off suddenly by----)

RADAR'S VOICE (over loudspeaker).   'Tenshun!
    All personnel report to assignments.   This is
    an alert.   The whirly-birds are on their way.
    Repeat--this is an alert.   (A communal sigh
    goes up.   The siren wails, LIGHTS DIM.)

(In the darkness HO-JON, DEVINE, KOREAN
    WOMAN #1 and KOREAN WOMAN #2 move to the
    edge of the stage with flashlights, their move-
    ments mingled in with the cast members who
    are EXITING R and L.)

DEVINE.   Hear anything, HO-JON?
HO-JON.   No, Sergeant.   I am not Radar Reilly.
DEVINE.   What a time for an alert.   (Pause; then.)
KOREAN WOMAN #2.   I hear them.   (She flashes
    on her light.)
KOREAN WOMAN #1.   I hear.   (She flashes on her light.)
DEVINE.   How many?
HO-JON.   Hard to tell.   (Sound of helicopters
    building.)   Always too many.   (He snaps on his
    light.)
DEVINE.   Just make sure the beams keep moving.
    (He turns on his flashlight.)
HO-JON (yelling into the night).   This way!   (The
    flashlight beams hit the ceiling of the theatre.
    Extra lights can be brought on if desired.   It's
    a repeat of the earlier flashlight sequence.)
ALL (ad lib).
        Over here!
        This way!
        Ya-hoo!
        Here!   Down here!
        Hey Joey!
        Etc.
(The flashlights move off DR, sound of helicopters
    grows fainter and fainter.)

ACT ONE
Scene Ten

CURTAIN OPENS. In "The Swamp," RADAR has his ear to the floor. FATHER MULCAHY appears in "Avenue A" coming from UR, behind the nurses' tent. WALT is in the mess tent, slumped over table, his face buried in his arms. FATHER MULCAHY enters "The Swamp" from right.)

RADAR (looking up). Digging in the belly of some Australian. They brought him in last night, full of shrapnel.

FATHER MULCAHY. Huh?

RADAR. Hawkeye and Duke. You were going to ask me where they were.

FATHER MULCAHY. You're a marvel, Radar. I have sad news.

RADAR. You mean about Ho-Jon?

FATHER MULCAHY. How did you know? (Thinks.) Oh, yes, I forgot about your gift.

RADAR. Heard the orders phoned in from Seoul. They came through Colonel Blake's office.

FATHER MULCAHY (sitting on cot). What a pity.

(TRAPPER ENTERS DR and crosses to right of "The Swamp," enters.)

RADAR (getting up). Nothing else worth hearing.
    All routine stuff.
FATHER MULCAHY. You might have a career in
    night clubs. Or a circus. Man with your ears
    could go places.
RADAR. None of that for me. I'm set for life.
TRAPPER (flopping down on his cot). How come?
RADAR. Sergeant Devine's gonna fix me up.
TRAPPER. Devine? He'll sell you a piece of the
    Brooklyn Bridge.
RADAR. I'm too smart for any of that. I bought
    his uranium stock, instead.

(DUKE ENTERS from UL taking off a surgical mask
    and smock. He enters "The Swamp" from left.)

DUKE. I'm bushed.
TRAPPER. Grim tidings.
DUKE. What is?
RADAR. The South Korean Army has drafted Ho-Jon,
    sir.
DUKE (as news sinks in). It can't be true.
TRAPPER. Rotten luck.
FATHER MULCAHY. Colonel Blake says there's
    nothing he can do about it.
TRAPPER. Not much he would do if he could.
    Ho-Jon's of age.

(HAWKEYE ENTERS from UL, moves down to the
    stage left entrance of "The Swamp," enters.)

HAWKEYE. Hi-y'all.
DUKE. They drafted Ho-Jon. Can you believe it?
HAWKEYE. They couldn't. He's not an American
    citizen.
DUKE. Not the American Army, you dummy. The
    Korean.

HAWKEYE. They can't do this to us! All the other
    houseboys in this unit combined aren't worth one
    of him.
FATHER MULCAHY. Can't be helped.

(While they talk, HO-JON appears in "Avenue A"
    from UR, coming behind the nurses' tent. He
    carries a small parcel holding his belongings
    and some books. Slowly, he walks down to "The
    Swamp" and enters. The others notice him,
    stand.)

HAWKEYE. There has to be something we can do.
DUKE. Let's talk to Colonel Blake.
HO-JON. Oh, no, Captains, sirs. I must go. It
    is only right. It is my duty. (The books.)
    Here are the books you let me read. (HO-JON
    sets down the parcel and takes out the books,
    hands them to DUKE.) I thank you for them.
DUKE. Any time. I'll -- I'll keep 'em for you,
    Ho-Jon.
HAWKEYE. We'll be thinking about you.
HO-JON. Thank you, sir.

(KOREANS, knowing HO-JON is soon to depart,
    ENTER DR, move into "Avenue A" and stand
    outside "The Swamp," R.)

DUKE. You take care of yourself, hear?
HO-JON. I will take care of myself, bring credit
    to my father's name, and, some day, I hope to
    be -- doctor like the honorable gentleman of the
    double natural. (TRAPPER, HAWKEYE, DUKE,
    RADAR, FATHER MULCAHY are visibly
    touched. HO-JON extends his hand.) Good-bye,
    Captain Hawkeye.
HAWKEYE (shaking hands). Good-bye, Ho-Jon.

HO-JON. Good-bye, Captain McIntyre.

TRAPPER (shaking hands). Make 'em sweat, soldier.

HO-JON. Good-bye, Captain Pierce.

DUKE (shaking hands). Ho-Jon.

HO-JON. Father. (FATHER MULCAHY shakes
    hands.) See ya, Radar.

RADAR (friendly wave). See ya, Ho-Jon. (HO-JON
    walks right of tent, bows to the Swampmen,
    EXITS into "Avenue A," goes off UR, KOREANS
    following after him.)

HAWKEYE. Sure hate to see that kid go.

DUKE. Got me with that doctor bit. I never knew
    he had that in the back of his mind. (HAWKEYE,
    DUKE and TRAPPER sit on their bunks, low in
    spirits. FATHER MULCAHY and RADAR EXIT
    into "Avenue A" and off DR.)

(DEVINE, carrying a tray of food, ENTERS from
    rear of mess tent, sees WALT, puts tray
    on the counter and crosses to his slumped-over
    form.)

DEVINE. Captain Waldowski, what's the matter?

WALT. Go away, leave me alone.

DEVINE. You sick or something?

WALT. Leave me alone, I said.

DEVINE (to himself). Oh, no, not again! (DEVINE
    exits mess tent, enters "Avenue C.") Hawkeye,
    Duke! (In "The Swamp," HAWKEYE, DUKE
    and TRAPPER look up. DEVINE enters the
    tent from left.) He's doing it again.

TRAPPER. Huh?

DEVINE. Captain McIntyre, it's Captain Waldowski.
    He's having one of his depressions. (The
    Swampmen are upset; temporarily they forget
    the letdown over the now gone HO-JON.)

DUKE. Oh, great.

HAWKEYE. But he had his month's depression last
    week. He's not due for another depression for
    three more weeks.
DEVINE. Somebody better tell him to take a look
    at the calendar.
TRAPPER (standing). Know what that means? No
    bingo games again, no poker games. Walt's
    the only guy who'll let the whole of MASH in his
    tent twenty-four hours a day.
DUKE. His depressions only last a few days.
TRAPPER. And he isn't good for much. When he's
    like that, Blake has to tie him to his drill.
DUKE. Trapper John, you go with the Sergeant and
    bring him back.
TRAPPER. Right. (TRAPPER and DEVINE exit
    into "Avenue C" and on into the mess tent.)
HAWKEYE. He won't do anything but lay in his sack
    and stare at the light bulb.
DUKE. We have to snap him out of this nonsense
    once and for all.
HAWKEYE. Any suggestions?
DUKE. Think, man, think.
HAWKEYE. I am thinking. One of these days Henry
    is going to have enough and ship Walt back to
    the States, and if that happens we're likely to
    get a joker like Burns to take his place. (Eyes
    brighten.) Wait a minute.
DUKE. What've you got?
HAWKEYE. Shock therapy.
DUKE. What?
HAWKEYE. Walt's drastic condition calls for drastic
    action.

(While this discussion is going on, TRAPPER and
DEVINE have pulled a dead-weight WALT from
the mess tent and guided him to the stage left
entrance of "The Swamp.")

TRAPPER. I'll take care of him from here on in.
    Thanks, Sergeant.
DEVINE. Yes, sir. Any time. (DEVINE EXITS
    UL and off. WALT stands in the stage left
    entry like a shell-shock victim, supported by
    TRAPPER.)
DUKE. Hiya, Walt, ole buddy-buddy.
HAWKEYE (pulling out a foot locker). Have a seat,
    Walt.
DUKE. Make yourself comfortable. How about a
    cool drink? Dr. Pepper? Squirt? (TRAPPER
    pulls WALT to the foot locker and sets him down.)

(BRIDGET ENTERS UR into "Avenue A" and crosses
    to stage right entrance of "The Swamp.")

HAWKEYE. What's the matter, Walt? (WALT
    stares deadpan into audience.)
BRIDGET. Female approaching! (She enters "The
    Swamp.") Hey, Walt, everyone's waiting for
    you over at the Poker Parlor. (Sees something's
    wrong.) What's the matter, Walt?
ALL. Sssssh.
BRIDGET. What I say, what I say?
WALT (flat). Life stinks.
HAWKEYE. Now, Walt, you don't mean that.
DUKE. Every day is a new day.
WALT. That's what I said. Life stinks.
HAWKEYE. Think of the beauty of each dawn.
TRAPPER. The joy of each sunset. (WALT sticks
    out his tongue and makes a raspberry in response
    to these Pollyannaisms. The others are not
    sure how to handle him this time.)
BRIDGET (motherly). Remember last time you said
    you were going to retreat from the world? That
    was only a passing thing. You're over-sensitive,
    that's all.

DUKE. Sure. (WALT isn't buying.)

WALT. I think you oughta know.

HAWKEYE. Know what?

WALT. I'm going to commit suicide.

BRIDGET. Again?

TRAPPER (taking WALT'S hand). We'll miss you, Walt.

DUKE. I hope you'll be happy in your new location.

HAWKEYE. How about leaving me your record player?

BRIDGET. You should give Colonel Blake a little warning, so he can get a replacement.

DUKE. How do you figure to go?

HAWKEYE. You could do the .45 between the eyebrows.

BRIDGET. That's been overdone, Hawkeye. I'd suggest something a bit more refined. (To an outsider not accustomed to the MASH *joie de vivre*, the joking and kidding might appear outrageous. But the MASH team has been through this many times before with WALT. Although they make their remarks tongue-in-cheek, WALT is serious.)

WALT. What would you suggest?

HAWKEYE. The .45 will do it. No question about that.

TRAPPER. That could get awfully sloppy.

HAWKEYE. How about a black capsule?

WALT. What's that?

HAWKEYE. It's a never-miss. Easy, pleasant, no side effects. You'll wake up in eternity.

WALT. Won't be any pain, will there? I can't stand pain. That's why I became a dentist.

DUKE. Figures.

HAWKEYE. The first thing you know you'll be listening to a heavenly chorus singing your high school victory song.

WALT. We didn't have one.

BRIDGET. Anybody got a black capsule?

HAWKEYE. We're going to get one right now.
(HAWKEYE motions for DUKE to follow him out
the tent, right. BRIDGET and TRAPPER stay
by the world-weary WALT to comfort. HAWKEYE
moves down into "Avenue A.")

DUKE (following). What are you talking about?
Black capsule?

HAWKEYE. Look, Walt's our friend. We gotta get
him out of this rut for good.

DUKE. Black capsule?

HAWKEYE. We'll knock him out for about twelve
hours and when he wakes up we'll scare him back
into a love of life.

DUKE. Better have something around in case he
looks like he won't wake up.

HAWKEYE. Duke, my boy, you worry too much.
(HAWKEYE EXITS DR.)

DUKE (calling after him). Tell that to Waldowski!
(He follows after HAWKEYE.)

BLACKOUT

(The TRAVELLER CURTAIN closes.)

ACT ONE
Scene Eleven

(Desk and chair for General Hammond are set DR,
    and the desk and chair for Colonel Blake, DL.
    In the darkness we hear the voice of GENERAL
    HAMMOND.)

GENERAL HAMMOND. . . . Operator. . . .
    Operator, are you still there? (Pause.) Well, snap
    it up. (Pause again.) I said--I said snap it up.
    This is vital. (Telephone rings on Colonel Blake's
    desk once--twice--three times.)

(The LIGHTS DIM UP. PVT. BOONE, munching a
    sandwich, saunters in from DL, picks up the
    receiver. Since his mouth is stuffed with food
    it's almost impossible to understand what he's
    saying.)

BOONE. The 4077th Mobile Army Surgical Hospital,
    Colonel Blake's office. Private Boone speaking.
    (GENERAL HAMMOND pulls the telephone from
    his ear, startled.)
GENERAL HAMMOND. Henry, Henry, that you?
    (BOONE takes another bite, makes another
    mumbled reply.)
BOONE. The 4077th Mobile Army Surgical Hospital.
    Colonel Blake's---- (In frustration, HAMMOND

slams down the receiver and taps the knobs.
BOONE hangs up.)

GENERAL HAMMOND. Operator, operator--look,
you knucklehead, you must have connected me
with one of the U.N. outfits. Couldn't understand
a word. I want Colonel Blake. Colonel Henry
Blake. Connect me! (BOONE leans on the edge
of the desk finishing his sandwich. Telephone
rings again--three times. BOONE picks it up.
GENERAL HAMMOND shrieks into it before
BOONE can speak.) Henry! (Startled, BOONE
drops the telephone.)

(BLAKE, a wild smoking jacket on over his uniform,
ENTERS DL.)

BLAKE. Boone, I thought I told you to get me some
shaving cream at the PX.
GENERAL HAMMOND. Henry!
BOONE. The telephone rang.
BLAKE. Well, answer it.
BOONE. I did, sir.
BLAKE. Then why is it on the floor?
GENERAL HAMMOND. Henry, Henry----
BOONE. I dropped it.
BLAKE (exasperated). Well, pick it up. Never mind.
Get me that shaving cream. And don't trip on
your way out. (BOONE EXITS, tripping on his
way out. BLAKE shouts after him.) Lime-
scented. I don't want it if it's not lime-scented.
Don't get orange like the last time. Gave me
pimples.
GENERAL HAMMOND. Lime? Orange? Hello,
hello, Henry? Hello, hello----(BLAKE picks
up the receiver, speaks with a smooth, professional voice.)
BLAKE. This is Colonel Henry Blake speaking.

Who am I speaking with, please?

GENERAL HAMMOND. Thank heaven I got you.

BLAKE. Who did you say this is?

GENERAL HAMMOND. This is General Hammond!
(BLAKE was biting a fingernail so he didn't hear.)
You wouldn't believe these phone connections.
First the operator connected me with a Turkish or
Greek unit. Couldn't get a syllable. Then the wires
crossed and I got some supply sergeant ordering a
crate of citrus. Oranges and limes. Now, listen,
Henry, this is serious.

BLAKE. Oh, it's you, General Hammond.

GENERAL HAMMOND. Of course it's me! (Deep
breath.) I tell you, Henry, you and your MASH team
will have me bananas before this conflict's over.

BLAKE. What can I do for you, General?

GENERAL HAMMOND. You can listen to me. That's
what you can do. I'm only going to say this once.
We're in trouble. There's a congresswoman
heading your way.

BLAKE. Congresswoman?

GENERAL HAMMOND. Congresswoman Goldfarb, and
she means business. She's a V. I. P. Making a report. Give her the red carpet treatment. And,
Henry----

BLAKE (worried). Sir?

GENERAL HAMMOND. If anything goes wrong this time,
I swear on my Masonic pin, I'll cream you and every
MASH imbecile working under you. Do I make
myself clear?

BLAKE. What did you say her name was again?
Goldfinger?

GENERAL HAMMOND. Not Goldfinger--Goldfarb! (In
rage, GENERAL HAMMOND slams down the receiver. BLAKE has a worried look on his face----)

BLACKOUT

ACT ONE
Scene Twelve

(In the BLACKNESS the desks and chairs are
        struck and RADAR'S voice comes over the
        loudspeaker.)

RADAR'S VOICE. Attention--your attention, please.
        Due to unforeseen circumstances the usual
        Friday Night Bingo and Potato Chip Frolic in
        the Painless Polish Poker Parlor and Dental
        Clinic has been canceled. Those of you who
        purchased bingo cards in advance are asked to
        hold on to them until further notice. Also,
        players attempting to get into future bingo
        games with homemade or counterfeit cards will
        be refused admittance. This applies especially
        to Sergeant Devine. Your full cooperation would
        be appreciated and Radar Reilly, he of the
        occult gifts, really thanks you. (Macabre laugh.)
        Ha, ha, ha.

(THE TRAVELLER CURTAIN OPENS in the darkness.
        Slowly the LIGHTS DIM UP. It's a strange sight
        that greets us. In "The Swamp," the nurses
        are wearing white surgical gowns, their faces
        covered with masks and their hair tucked under
        operating caps. They are: BRIDGET, NANCY,

JANICE, LOUISE. The doctors are dressed in
similar fashion: TRAPPER, UGLY. All are
grouped around a long wooden box on the floor,
C. The overhead light now has a greenish bulb
and the effect is weird. HAWKEYE is working
on some infernal apparatus left of the long, low
box. The apparatus shoots off sparks, electrical
volts, makes a lot of noise. It's a scene out of
every monster film we've ever seen--with
HAWKEYE as the mad scientist and the others
as devoted, but equally mad, collaborators.
From DR comes DUKE, also in surgical garb
and carrying a lighted lantern. He's all bent
and twisted, imitating the mad doctor's ever-
faithful stooge, Igor. DUKE enters the tent
through stage right entrance and goes to the
wooden box, which looks suspiciously like a
coffin. He holds the lantern high and peers in.)

DUKE (imitating Igor). Good, good, master.
HAWKEYE. Quiet, you fool.
DUKE. He moved, master. He moved. (Nurses,
    doctors applaud softly.)
ALL (*ad libs*).
        Genius.
        Brilliant.
        Fantastic.
        Masterpiece.
    (HAWKEYE continues to juice up his crazy
    machine; more sparks, more noise.)
DUKE (jumping around). He opened an eye! An eye,
    master!
ALL. Ooooh--aaaah---- (Faint, scattered applause.)
HAWKEYE. Silence! (All quiet.) This will be my
    greatest achievement. To think that they laughed
    at me. Me! The greatest scientist the world
    has ever produced. (He goes back to his machine.)

(UR, from behind the nurses' tent into "Avenue A,"
     comes COLONEL BLAKE escorting Congress-
     woman GOLDFARB, a middle-aged type,
     dressed in a heavy coat. BLAKE carries a
     brief case. They walk down into "Avenue B,"
     stage right of "The Swamp.")

GOLDFARB. Hope this isn't too much trouble for
     you, Colonel.
BLAKE. Delighted to show you about the compound,
     Congresswoman Goldfinger.
GOLDFARB. That's Goldfarb. I intend to make a
     full report of everything I see.
BLAKE. I'm sure you'll find everything in this
     MASH unit S.O.P. We're serious, dedicated
     professionals.
GOLDFARB. Splendid.
BLAKE (taking some paper from his brief case).
     Here's that report you asked for.
GOLDFARB (taking it, looking). Colonel Blake!
BLAKE (smiling). Ma'am?
GOLDFARB. This isn't a report. It's a bingo card.
     (BLAKE pulls it back and dives into the brief
     case, fishes out the correct paper, hands it to
     her. She glares at him, studies the report.)

(In "The Swamp" things are heating up.)

DUKE. Alive, master! He's alive!

(Groggily, WALT sits up in the coffin wondering why
     he doesn't hear that heavenly choir. He's
     wearing a Frankenstein mask and his fatigue
     jacket is on backwards.)

WALT. Where--where am I?
HAWKEYE. My laboratory.

WALT. W--w--what?

HAWKEYE. Don't you understand, Walter? I've
    brought you back from the dead!

WALT. Me? (Spooky applause from doctors and
    nurses who resemble a bizarre chorus of
    medical fiends.)

ALL (*ad lib*).
        Back from the dead.
        He walks.
        He talks.
        He's alive.
        Etc.
    (All this is too much for WALT. Terrified he
    feels the mask which, in his semi-drugged state,
    must feel like his own flesh.)

WALT. My face--my face--what's happened to my
    face? (One of the nurses holds out a big mirror
    and WALT stares into it, seeing only the re-
    flection of the Frankenstein monster mask.)
    No! No! No! (He leaps from the coffin and
    flees "The Swamp" toward left, crosses around
    into "Avenue B" and runs smack into Congress-
    woman GOLDFARB.) No! No! No!

GOLDFARB. Eeeeeeeek! (WALT, frightened by
    her scream, runs off into "Avenue C" and
    disappears from sight UL. BLAKE is dumb-
    founded. Congresswoman GOLDFARB points
    after the fleeing WALT.) What--what was that
    "thing"?

BLAKE (faking a smile). Our local dentist. He's a
    bit odd. (Congresswoman GOLDFARB faints
    into BLAKE'S arms.)

    (In "The Swamp," the medicos are congratulating
    HAWKEYE and DUKE.)

ALL (*ad lib*).
> Good work, guys.
> Congratulations, Hawkeye.
> Great Igor, Duke.
> Etc.

CURTAIN

ACT TWO
Scene One

The CURTAIN OPENS revealing a few KOREANS
and G. I. 's, coming and going in the compound.
Main attention is on the nurses' tent. Here we
find BRIDGET, NANCY and LOUISE. RADAR
is "listening" in "The Swamp, " ear to the floor.
NANCY is softly singing some of "If I Had the
Wings of an Angel. " MARGARET ENTERS the
nurses' tent from UR.)

MARGARET. Good morning, ladies. (NANCY
stops singing and BRIDGET and LOUISE tense.
Visits from MARGARET HOULIHAN are not
common.)

BRIDGET. Good morning, Major.

LOUISE. Ma'am.

MARGARET. And how are we all this morning?

NANCY. Fine, ma'am.

MARGARET. Everyone staying fit? Hmmmm?

BRIDGET. Yes, Major.

MARGARET. Good, good. I'll come to the point.
I have written a letter.

NANCY (without thinking). Not another one. (BRIDG-
ET tries to shush her.)

MARGARET. Yes, Lieutenant Phillips--another one.

NANCY. Beg pardon, ma'am.

MARGARET. I should think so. (Then:) Pointless

to file any complaint with Lieutenant-Colonel
Blake. He either ignores what I have to say or
consigns it to File Number Thirteen.

LOUISE. The wastebasket.

MARGARET. Exactly. This time I am making my
complaint directly to General Hammond.

BRIDGET. You'd go over the Colonel's head?

MARGARET. He's left me no choice.

(In "The Swamp," RADAR sits up, a terrified
expression on his face.)

RADAR. Golly!

BRIDGET. I take it your complaint is about the
boys.

MARGARET. If by "the boys" you mean Hawkeye
Pierce and Duke Forrest you're absolutely
correct. Their soldierly bearing is shock-
ing. They have no more regard for the military code than I do for a racing form. Their
conduct is inexcusable. Have you heard
what they did in Japan?

LOUISE. They won a golf tournament.

MARGARET. They arrived for a serious operation dressed in Bermuda shorts and sneak-
ers--with the toes cut out! The tournament was
later. The M.P.'s had to escort them back to
the air field. They were A.W.O.L. when they
played in the tournament.

BRIDGET. But the patient did survive. The one in
Tokyo?

MARGARET. Nothing to do with the issue. You know
how they regard the nurses here. Common cour-
tesy isn't in their vocabulary and I, for one,
strongly resent being referred to as--I can hardly
bring myself to say it--"Hot Lips."

NANCY. But what can we do about it, Major?

MARGARET. As women we can stand together.
    I'm asking that each of you sign my complaint.
    (The nurses don't like this idea at all.)
BRIDGET. With your permission, ma'am.
MARGARET. Say what you will.
BRIDGET. I can't defend their personal conduct.
    I'm not even going to try. I don't think their
    personal conduct really matters.
MARGARET. What?
BRIDGET. They're two of the finest doctors I've
    ever worked with. They know what they're
    doing and how to do it. And they save lives.
    That's all that's important, isn't it?
MARGARET. Is it?
NANCY. They're not Regular Army. They didn't
    ask to be here.
LOUISE. They were drafted.
MARGARET. Beside the point. They're soldiers.
LOUISE. Soldiers first and doctors second?
MARGARET. Obviously, I've been mistaken about
    how we all feel. I thought your devotion to the
    ideals of Army nursing----
BRIDGET. They're really not so bad, Major. Con-
    sidering all the sweat and blood they go through,
    it's a miracle they're as good as they are.
MARGARET. I can't argue against their compe-
    tency. In the operating tent it's above reproach.
    But, they set a bad example in other ways and
    eventually it will work against us all. If only
    they weren't so----
BRIDGET. Fresh?
MARGARET. In any case, you refuse to sign?
NANCY. We can't, ma'am.
MARGARET. You mean you won't. Very well. I
    shall contact the General over my own signa-
    ture and mine alone. (She EXITS UR and off.)

(RADAR, in "The Swamp," stands.)

RADAR. Better tell Trapper John about this.
(He hurries out left entrance into "Avenue C,"
up around the mess tent, and out. When the
stage picture is right, LOUISE and NANCY will
leave the nurses' tent UR and off.)

(JANICE ENTERS compound from DR just as UGLY
ENTERS from DL. She moves along "Avenue B.")

UGLY. Where are you going?
JANICE. Coffee.
UGLY. Don't mind if I do.
JANICE. We may have to make it ourselves. The
M.P.'s have Sergeant Devine.
UGLY. Again?
JANICE. Seems two different Koreans claim he sold
them fishing rights in the Bay of Rhum and now
they want their money back.
UGLY. Bay of Rhum, huh? He's branching out.
(Grins.) Thanks for knitting me those socks.
JANICE. Gets cold nights. Do they fit?
UGLY. If I knot 'em together and use 'em for a scarf.
JANICE. Ugly, do me a favor.
UGLY. Anything.
JANICE. Make that knot real tight.

(TRAPPER comes running around the corner of the
mess tent from UL into "Avenue C" and crosses
to JANICE and UGLY.)

TRAPPER. Boy, oh, boy. Know what Radar just
heard?
UGLY. Something about Hot Lips, I bet.
TRAPPER. On the button.
JANICE. Please don't call the Major by that name.

TRAPPER. She's a fire-belching dragon.

JANICE. It'll only make trouble.

TRAPPER. Made trouble already. (BRIDGET leaves nurses' tent DR, EXITS off stage.) Hot Lips is sending a detailed letter to General Hammond, going over Blake's head. She'll give names and dates, and a full description of every un-army thing Hawkeye and Duke have ever done. They could get broken for the things they've gotten away with.

UGLY. What are we gonna do, Trapper?

JANICE. Captain McIntyre, may I ask you a personal question?

TRAPPER. Shoot.

JANICE. Why do people call you "Trapper" John?

TRAPPER (blushing). I once trapped a college coed in a washroom.

JANICE (sour). Boyish prank, of course.

TRAPPER. I'm high-spirited by nature. What does any of that matter now? If Houlihan sends that letter, Hawkeye and Duke will be hurting.

UGLY. We could have Radar intercept it in the mail room.

JANICE. Not if she delivers it personally.

(WALT ENTERS from DR.)

WALT. Better get set.

TRAPPER. For what?

WALT. They're moving in casualties. A South Korean patrol. Bringing 'em up by stretcher bearers.

JANICE. And I was hoping to wash my hair.

UGLY. Looks nice dirty. (UGLY puts his arms around JANICE and gives her a hug. She EXITS UL with WALT. TRAPPER and UGLY EXIT DR.)

(The TRAVELLER CURTAIN closes.)

ACT TWO

Scene Two

BLAKE (voice, over loudspeaker). All personnel
    report to their assigned stations. This is an
    alert. Repeat--all personnel report to their
    assigned stations. Repeat--this is an alert.

(From DL, NURSES, KOREANS and G.I.'s cross to
    DR. JANICE and WALT ENTER DL and start
    across. FATHER MULCAHY is behind them.)

FATHER MULCAHY. Walt. (WALT and JANICE
    stop, turn.)
WALT. Yeah?
FATHER MULCAHY. I thought you'd want to know.
WALT. Know what?
FATHER MULCAHY. There's a friend of ours in
    with the casualties. I've just been with him.
WALT. Friend?
JANICE. Who?
FATHER MULCAHY. Ho-Jon. (WALT and JANICE
    are stunned.) Hawkeye and Duke are with him now.
JANICE. How does it look?
FATHER MULCAHY. Not good. (Heartsick at the
    news, JANICE and WALT start on their way when
    the building sound of artillery fire causes them
    to stop and look off into the distance. They're
    worried. FATHER MULCAHY turns back and
    EXITS DL.)

LIGHTS FADE

ACT TWO
Scene Three

THE TRAVELLER CURTAIN OPENS only part way.
We're in the operating tent, which is nothing
more than a canvas backing or large hospital
screen that blocks off a view of the compound.
There is an operating table centered for maximum view and the lighting is directed to this
small, confined area. A plasma bottle is
suspended from some rack. MARGARET is
assisting. HAWKEYE is by the table. UGLY,
in his role of anesthesiologist, has placed a
"mask" over HO-JON'S face and applies the
anesthetic. The tone of the scene is very
dramatic.)

HAWKEYE. Hang in there, Ho-Jon. We're here.
Duke will be along in a minute. You're in good
hands. (UGLY shakes his head to indicate the
Korean boy is almost gone.) Hang in there.
(Sound of distant artillery grows in volume and
underscores the scene.)

(DUKE, in surgical gown and mask, ENTERS.
HAWKEYE looks at him nervously.)

HAWKEYE (to UGLY). Can he hear anything at all?
(UGLY nods that he can.) Listen to me, Ho-Jon.

We need your help. You've got to fight, too.
You've got to give us all your strength. Listen,
Ho-Jon, you pull through and we'll get you to
medical school in the States. That's a promise.
Can you hear me? (DUKE touches HAWKEYE'S
arm, meaning let's get on with it.)

DUKE. Ready, nurse?

MARGARET. Ready, doctor. (Artillery up. The
operating personnel look up, concerned, then
set about their work.)

(In the dimly lighted areas DR and DL, outside the
operating tent, the KOREANS have gathered.
They stand almost in silhouette. One man wears
the traditional costume: white gown, tall black
hat, cane. KOREAN WOMAN #1 carries a
ceremonial bell which she rings from time to
time to discourage evil spirits. They are holding
a vigil for the dying HO-JON.

As the operation proceeds, sound of artillery
grows nearer and nearer. Once, the operating
lights dim dangerously. Medicos react, the
lights dim back up. The operation goes on.

Slowly, for effect, the lights grow dimmer and
dimmer until, at last, all is in blackness and
nothing is heard except an occasional burst of
shelling and the ringing of the Buddhist prayer
bell.)

(The TRAVELLER CURTAIN closes.)

ACT TWO
Scene Four

The LIGHTS COME UP bright and warm. MISS
RANDAZZLE, a young secretary, is standing
DR with pad and pencil poised for dictation.
She is dressed in New England fashion, which
is to say a plaid skirt, reserved blouse, single
strand of pearls. With her is DEAN MERCY
LODGE of Androscoggin College, Maine. She's
dressed in heavy tweeds and wears *pince-nez*
glasses and sensible shoes. Her hair is grey
or white and her backbone is made from steel.
She speaks with a Down East "twang. ")

MERCY. Ready, Miss Randazzle?
MS RANDAZZLE. Ready, Dean Lodge.
MERCY. Then let us proceed. (Dictates.) Dear
    Hawkeye.
MS RANDAZZLE. Hawkeye, did you say, Dean
    Lodge?
MERCY. Yes, Miss Randazzle. Hawkeye is what I
    said. He was before your time. (Continues.)
    Dear Hawkeye, your recent letter after all these
    years came as a complete surprise. I wish I
    could say I was delighted. Cautious will have
    to do.
MS RANDAZZLE. Cautious, Dean Lodge?
MERCY. Cautious, Miss Randazzle. And spell it
    with a "C" this time, not with a "K." (Continuing.)
    I naturally remember you very well, Hawkeye.

In fact, I shall never forget you. Not that I
haven't tried. In my job one has to take the
bitter with the sweet. You ask if I will accept
some Korean youngster as a pre-med student.
My natural expectation is that, if I acceded to
your request, I will soon have on my hands
some illiterate seventy-year-old refugee from
a leper colony. Despite the dim possibility you
might have matured slightly over the years,
that is really what I expect.

MS RANDAZZLE. He sounds like quite a character,
Dean Lodge.

MERCY. Hawkeye Pierce was a combination of Tom
Sawyer and Lucifer himself. (Back to business.
MS RANDAZZLE writes.) However, this sort
of humanitarianism is popular these days. If
you feel your boy can do college work and if
you can get him over here and supply him with
fifteen hundred dollars a year, we will give him
a chance. Underline that, Miss Randazzle--
a chance.(MS RANDAZZLE underlines.) En-
closed is an application for Ho-Jon to complete.
Sincerely, Mercy Lodge, Dean of Androscoggin
College. P. S. If this is some kind of Hawkeye
Pierce joke, I'll never again buy a lobster from
your father. Underline never. (MS RANDAZZLE
makes another underline.)

(LIGHTS FADE fast to BLACKNESS. Sound of
howling wind.)

ACT TWO
Scene Five

When the LIGHTS COME UP again, we're still in
front of the TRAVELLER CURTAIN. KOREAN
WOMAN #1 and KOREAN WOMAN #2, bundled
up warmly, heads low to fight the chilling blasts,
cross from DL to DR. RADAR and DEVINE,
wearing overcoats and hats to their ears, ENTER
DR and move DL.)

RADAR. I'm so cold my goosebumps have blue
veins.
DEVINE. Think warm.

(PVT. LOPEZ, excited, also in heavy clothes,
ENTERS DL.)

LOPEZ. I don't believe it! I don't believe it!
RADAR. Okay, Lopez, you don't believe it!
LOPEZ . But you haven't seen 'em.
RADAR. Seen who?
LOPEZ. Their jeep broke down! Right here at
MASH!
DEVINE. Goody for the jeep.
LOPEZ. Luck of the ole double natural is holding
up.
RADAR. I heard the jeep. So what?
DEVINE. I think the cold weather has frosted your

brain, Lopez. <u>What</u> are you babbling about?

LOPEZ. Three of the sweetest little entertainers
that Special Services ever discovered were on
their way up north and their jeep fell apart.

RADAR. Is that what you're all excited about?

DEVINE. You're still young, Lopez. I've seen
some of them entertainers. Beasties. Hair
like straw, skin like leather, teeth like nail
files.

RADAR. And they're all shaped like Sherman tanks.

LOPEZ. You don't want to meet 'em?

DEVINE. No offense, Lopez, but we'd rather be
introduced to Daffy Duck. (To RADAR.) Come
on, let's see what's on in the Painless Polish
Poker Parlor.

(DEVINE and RADAR turn back DR as the three
BONWIT SISTERS ENTER DL. Although it's a
trio, each of the girls, MITZI, FRITZI and
AGNES, looks and sounds exactly like the other
two. They're in their late teens but act younger.
In fact, their speech is almost baby talk. Their
hair style, blonde most likely, is very show
business, and they all look helpless and
"adorable." The sort of girls male chauvinists
will instinctively want to protect and women will
detest. To add to their considerable charms,
the sisters are wearing their tap dancing
costumes, pretty, gaudy affairs with fringe and
sparkles. Even though their footsies are encased
in awkward combat boots, they're freezing and
rubbing their arms and legs to stay warm.)

MITZI. 'Scuse us, Private Lopez, sir, but we
were getting so cold sitting in that nasty ole jeep.

FRITZI. If we all stayed in that jeep one more
minute we'd have turned baby blue for sure.

AGNES. So we got out of that little ole nasty jeep and
    came here for your protection, Private Lopez, sir.
    We're just helpless without a strong man around.
    (On the sound of those itty bitty Southern belle
    voices, RADAR and DEVINE turn around. They're
    bedazzled and stand with their mouths wide open
    in wonder. Never have they seen such beauty.
    Venuses stepped down from some Botticelli
    masterpiece.)
MITZI. I need a kleenex, Private Lopez.
FRITZI. I'm all numb--right to the top of my head.
AGNES. Ach-choo.
DEVINE (taking off his overcoat). What's the matter
    with you, Lopez?
RADAR. Insensitive oaf.
LOPEZ. Me? (DEVINE puts his overcoat around
    MITZI.)
DEVINE. There you go. Nice and comfy. (RADAR
    puts his coat around FRITZI. Following along,
    LOPEZ puts his coat around AGNES.)
AGNES. Oooooooh. It's so cozy in this great big
    man's overcoat.
MITZI. I knew some gentlemen would come to our
    rescue. They always do.
FRITZI (to RADAR). I'm going to give you a great
    big sugar. (FRITZI kisses RADAR on the cheek.)
RADAR. Wow!
DEVINE. Come on, girls. We've got to get you to
    some nice warm spot before you catch your
    death. (RADAR and DEVINE hustle the giggling
    BONWIT SISTERS off L. LOPEZ, cold without
    his overcoat, is left alone in front of the curtain.
    Sulking, he yells after DEVINE and RADAR.)
LOPEZ. Remind me to introduce you guys to Daffy
    Duck sometime!

ACT TWO
Scene Six

THE CURTAIN OPENS on the compound.

> HAWKEYE and TRAPPER are stretched out on their cots, napping. DUKE is sewing on a button to a shirt.

> In the mess tent BRIDGET, LOUISE, NANCY, grimy in dirty work clothes, their hair tucked under their fatigue caps, are having coffee. They're exhausted. KOREAN WOMAN #2 is behind the counter.)

NANCY. What I wouldn't give for a hot shower and a shampoo.

BRIDGET. Spigots are frozen. No hot water for a couple of days.

LOUISE (checking her nails). I had to cut my nails back again. Getting too sharp for the surgical gloves.

NANCY. Listen.

BRIDGET. What?

LOUISE. I didn't hear anything. (Now there comes the offstage giggles of the BONWIT SISTERS and ad lib comments of RADAR, DEVINE and LOPEZ.)

BRIDGET. I hear something now.

NANCY. Sounds like a bunch of tropical birds.

(The nurses turn to entrance as RADAR, LOPEZ
    and DEVINE usher in the BONWIT SISTERS.)

MITZI (looking around). Ooooooh. What a nice little
    restaurant-poo. (She giggles at what she thought
    was an amusing observation.)
FRITZI. Can I get a cheeseburger?
DEVINE. Anything your little hearts desire. Sit
    down, girls, make yourselves to home.
    (DEVINE goes behind the counter and busies
    himself, sending KOREAN WOMAN #2 out for
    some supplies. RADAR and LOPEZ rush the
    BONWITS to the downstage table, which happens
    to be where the nurses are sitting. In their
    enthusiasm, RADAR and LOPEZ push the nurses
    aside and plop down the BONWITS. The nurses
    stand aside, angry.)
BRIDGET. What is this, Private?
LOPEZ. Entertainers from Special Services. Their
    jeep broke down.
RADAR. Girls, I'd like to have you meet Lieutenant
    Kimble, Captain McCarthy, and Lieutenant
    Phillips.
AGNES. We're very happy to meet you gentlemen.
    (The nurses are speechless. They look at their
    sexless, masculine fatigues and quickly take off
    their caps and let their hair loose.)
FRITZI. Oh, look, Mitzi. Isn't that interesting?
    They're women.
MITZI. Sort of.
BRIDGET (icy). And what is it you do in Special
    Services? (Sarcastic.) Ladies.
AGNES. Tap dance.
NANCY (can't believe it). Could we hear that again?
FRITZI. Tap dance.

MITZI. We can tap dance faster than any other
     person on the face of this earth.

AGNES. Or any other place.

FRITZI. Including South Korea. (The nurses look
     at each other in dismay. What a bunch of pea-
     brains.)

MITZI. Would you like to see us? I mean, after
     all, that's what we're in Korea for.

LOUISE. What are you in Korea for? (MITZI
     stands, forces herself to repeat something she
     had a hard time memorizing.)

MITZI. Uh, uh--quote--"To keep everybody happy
     and morale high--uh, uh--to increase the fighting
     efficiency of our troops and,at the same time--
     uh, uh--remain committed to the ideals of
     democracy." Unquote. (The nurses applaud
     faintly. MITZI sits.)

BRIDGET. How long did it take you to memorize
     that, dear?

MITZI. There's more. (Like a three-year-old.)
     But I don't really understand it.

BRIDGET. Perhaps it's just as well. For democracy,
     I mean.

AGNES. 'Course we should have our piano man and
     our drummer but they went on ahead, so if
     you'll all hum or sing, we'll do our best.

RADAR. Anything, Mitzi.

AGNES. I'm Agnes. (Points.) She's Mitzi.

FRITZI. I'm Fritzi, silly. (She points.) She's
     Mitzi. (The BONWITS giggle loudly, thinking
     they're very humorous.)

LOPEZ. What do you want us to sing?

BRIDGET. How about "Empty Saddles in the Old
     Corral."

AGNES (pouting). Can't tap dance to that. Any idiot
     knows that. (BRIDGET and the other nurses are
     steaming.)

RADAR. How about "Give My Regards to Broadway"?
AGNES. I was just going to suggest that. How did
    you know?
RADAR. It's a gift.
DEVINE. Music, maestro, please. (DEVINE,
    RADAR and LOPEZ begin to sing. MITZI,
    FRITZI and AGNES stand and remove their
    overcoats.)
THE MEN.
        Give my regards to Broadway,
        Remember me to Herald Square;
        Tell all the gang at Forty-second Street
        That I will soon be there.
        Whisper of how I'm yearning
        To mingle with the old-time throng;
        Give my regards to old Broadway
        And say that I'll be there ere long.
    (BONWIT SISTERS are into their routine, all
    toothy smiles. Their "act" is wretched, made
    all the more terrible by the boots and the girls'
    obvious lack of talent.)

    (In "The Swamp" HAWKEYE and TRAPPER sit
    up, wondering what's going on in the mess tent.)

        "Give my regards to Broadway . . . "
        Etc.
    (The nurses are appalled by the amateurishness
    of the dancers, the silliness of the girls, and
    the slavish behavior of the enlisted men. The
    "act" finishes in a stagey "hands-out-for-applause"
    finale. The men applaud wildly and ad lib.)
        Bravo!
        Encore, encore!
        More, more!
BRIDGET (when the acclaim dies out). That has to
    be the worse act I've ever seen.

FRITZI (offended). Oh.

MITZI. Pay no attention to them, Fritzi.

AGNES. They hate us because we're young.

LOUISE. What do you think we are--Grandma Moses?
     (The BONWITS lean to LOPEZ and RADAR
     for protection against the "nasty" nurses.
     DEVINE comes out from behind the counter.)

BRIDGET. Let's get out of this--"restaurant-poo."

NANCY (moving to exit). Why couldn't it have been
     Elvis Presley's jeep that broke down? (By
     now, TRAPPER, HAWKEYE and DUKE are
     standing at the stage left entrance to "The
     Swamp," staring off in the direction of the mess
     tent.)

          (The TRAVELLER CURTAIN closes.)

ACT TWO

Scene Seven

MARGARET and JANICE ENTER DR.)

MARGARET. I'll stay overnight at Headquarters.
    My appointment with General Hammond is for
    nine in the morning.
JANICE. Yes, Major.
MARGARET. If Colonel Blake should ask for my
    whereabouts you may tell him. I tried to see
    him, but Private Boone couldn't locate him. Or
    said he couldn't.
JANICE. He was in Captain Waldowski's tent.
MARGARET. As usual.

(LOUISE and NANCY ENTER from DL.)

MARGARET. Lieutenant Kimble?
NANCY (crossing over). Ma'am?
MARGARET. You'll assist Captains Pierce and
    Forrest if any case comes into surgery.
NANCY. You won't be here?
MARGARET. I'll be with the General. I understand
    "the boys" are taking up a collection for some-
    thing or other.
NANCY. Yes, ma'am. It's for----
MARGARET (cutting her off). Don't bother to
    explain. If they're taking up a collection, it's

for something to their benefit. And undoubtedly
questionable. (MARGARET EXITS briskly DL.)

NANCY. That "questionable" collection is money
for Ho-Jon's trip to the States. Hawkeye tossed
in his month's pay, ditto for Duke, but it's
not nearly enough.

JANICE. We've got problems of our own.

LOUISE. You mean the Bonwits?

JANICE. I mean the nitwits.

NANCY. Who do those men think they are? They
treat us like doormats and when those dancing
mice show up mouthing baby talk, they act as
if royalty were in town.

JANICE. Men are so silly.

NANCY. We shouldn't let them get away with it.

LOUISE. What can we do?

JANICE. Ask ourselves what Duke and Hawkeye
would do.

NANCY. Formulate a plan.

LOUISE. And then?

NANCY. Action.

JANICE. We owe it to our pride.

LOUISE. I've been here a year and Sergeant Devine
never made a cheeseburger for me.

NANCY. Remember, girls, revenge is not only
sweet--it's therapeutic.

LOUISE and JANICE. Hear, hear.

NANCY. At least the male officers have more
sense. (NANCY turns and EXITS DL, followed
by a determined JANICE and LOUISE.)

ACT TWO
Scene Eight

THE TRAVELLER CURTAIN OPENS revealing the
BONWIT SISTERS in "The Swamp." Foot
lockers have been pushed together to make a
table and over the foot lockers is a tablecloth,
and lighted candles. The dancers have attractive
kimonos over their dance costumes, but still
wear heavy boots. They are sitting on pillows
around the "table," dining. HAWKEYE, UGLY,
DUKE, TRAPPER JOHN and WALT hover
around, each with a dish from which they serve
their guests. The whole thing resembles an
elegant Oriental restaurant.)

UGLY (holding up a bottle). More mineral water?
MITZI. Goodness gracious, no. I'm already water-
     logged. Hee, hee.
TRAPPER. More rice?
FRITZI. No, no. Any more and we'll turn into
     rice kernels. (The girls giggle uproariously.)
DUKE. Witty things.
HAWKEYE. How about a Mr. Goodbar?
AGNES. We surely do want to thank you boys for
     these fetching kimonos.
WALT. Think nothing of it. I bought them from one
     of the Korean women in the compound. She
     makes 'em, models 'em, too. Just your size.
MITZI. You boys are scumptious.

FRITZI. Scumptious-wumptious.

(BRIDGET comes into "Avenue A" from around
        nurses' tent and walks to the stage right entrance.)

BRIDGET. Female approaching!
AGNES. One of those horrid ole nurse ladies.
        (BRIDGET enters tent, reacts to banquet scene.)
BRIDGET. If I had known, I'd have dressed formal.
WALT. The girls aren't used to our harsh way of
        life. Besides, the enlisted men don't have the
        proper know-how when it comes to entertaining
        important civilians.
BRIDGET (unimpressed). And you do, I suppose.
MITZI. Everyone here is so nice, we're gonna stay
        a few days, put on our performance, and bring
        a bit of hometown America into your dreary lives.
BRIDGET. We didn't know just how miserable we
        were until you ladies showed up. (To Swampmen.)
        You gents better get your dreary lives over to
        the Colonel's office. Big doings.
DUKE (worried). Could it be Houlihan's letter?
BRIDGET. One way to find out.

(The Swampmen file out right entrance, into "Avenue
        A," and out, DR. As soon as they're out,
        JANICE, LOUISE and NANCY appear from DL,
        cross to left of "The Swamp," enter.)

MITZI. I thought this tent was reserved for male
        officers. Exclusively.
AGNES. So did I.
FRITZI. Likewise, I'm sure.
NANCY. We want to apologize for the way we acted
        in the mess hall.
MITZI (pouting). You weren't very nice.
FRITZI. Seeing as how we gave up a week's

engagement in Bayonne, New Jersey, to come
here.

AGNES. And share your hardships with you. (Nurses
eye the "hardship" table.)

JANICE. I'm sorry for you girls. You have such
lovely skin.

MITZI. Why, thank you, honey. We use lemons
and cold creams and----(Thinks, then:) Sorry?

LOUISE. Didn't anyone tell you?

BRIDGET. You're in a high-risk area,
dermatologically speaking.

MITZI. Derma--derma--?

LOUISE. Dermatology.

FRITZI. Sounds awful. What is it?

BRIDGET. Skin rash.

JANICE. They've written it up in the medical journals.
They call it "Mash Blotch."

AGNES. Mash Blotch?

NANCY. Once you get it you can't get rid of it.
It's all over my back. Would you like to see?
(NANCY makes to show her back. BONWITS
are horrified.)

BONWITS. No, no.

MITZI. Things like that upset me. I'm delicate.

NANCY. The severe cases require isolation.

LOUISE. Sometimes it covers the face completely.
Breaks out in violent purple. (BONWITS are
going into shock.)

JANICE. Comes from the locale here. The water
and the food we eat. (BONWITS look at their
plates in horror.)

FRITZI. Food?

AGNES. Ugh.

BRIDGET. Even clothes are contaminated.
(BONWITS, numb, look at the kimonos in a daze.)

LOUISE. Shake hands with any one of us and you
might as well be embracing a bush of poison oak.

JANICE (to MITZI). Oh, look. See that? You got
     the start of a Mash Blotch on your jaw line.
MITZI (terrified).   Let's get out of this terrible place.
FRITZI. Hurry. (BONWITS are heading out into
     "Avenue A.")

(TRAPPER, UGLY and WALT ENTER from DR.)

WALT. Why'd Bridget go and tell us the Colonel
     wanted to see us? Some joke. (They see the
     BONWITS fleeing "The Swamp" in panic.)
UGLY. Where you going?
WALT. You haven't had dessert.
TRAPPER. Let's go over to the Poker Parlor. We
     can dance cheek to cheek. (He starts toward
     them, arms out for an embrace.)
BONWITS. Aaaaah! (Fearful the men might touch them
     and thus communicate the horrible medical phenome-
     non, the BONWITS dash off DL, flinging off the
     kimonos as they run.)
UGLY. What do you make of that?

     (Inside "The Swamp," BRIDGET, NANCY, JANICE
     and LOUISE have seated themselves at the "table.")

WALT. They acted like we had poison oak or something.
UGLY. Maybe we've been away from home too long.
     (They stare off in the distance after the BONWITS.
     They scratch their heads, wondering what's gone
     wrong.)

     (The nurses are eating with gusto.)

BRIDGET. Pass the rice.

(LIGHTS FADE to darkness. TRAVELLER CURTAIN
     closes.)

ACT TWO
Scene Nine

LIGHTS COME UP, revealing DEAN MERCY LODGE
DR, dictating another letter to MISS RANDAZZLE.)

MERCY. Dear Hawkeye, while I appreciate your
enthusiasm in recommending your Korean protege,
I must repeat that under no circumstances can
he be accepted at Androscoggin until all his
financial obligations, at least for the first year,
are met. We have received Ho-Jon's----

MS RANDAZZLE. Ho-Jon, Dean Lodge?

MERCY. Ho-Jon, Miss Randazzle.

MS RANDAZZLE. Ho as in "ho-ho-ho."

MERCY (sighing). Correct.

MS RANDAZZLE (making a correction). Ho-Jon. I
have it.

MERCY. We have received Ho-Jon's application and
his record appears to be outstanding, although
somewhat unusual. The letter accompanying
his application was particularly impressive and
influenced our decision to accept him. My
suggestion that you might have written it for him
was quickly squelched by members of the English
Department who remember you. Nevertheless,
we look forward to Ho-Jon's arrival. Very truly
yours, etc. Got that, Miss Randazzle?

MS RANDAZZLE. What if they don't raise the tuition

money?

MERCY. Then Ho-Jon stays in Korea. Come along;
    faculty meeting at two.

(Emphasis shifts to DL where Blake's desk and chair
    have been set up in the Blackout. MERCY and
    MS RANDAZZLE have EXITED. BLAKE is
    shuffling some papers.)

BLAKE. Boone! Where's my fly swatter!

    (BOONE dashes in from DL.)

BOONE. Sir?

BLAKE. Where's my fly swatter?

BOONE. Don't you remember? You broke it on my
    helmet liner.

BLAKE. I do not remember. Get me another one.

(BOONE moves R, sees DUKE coming in from DR.)

BOONE (turning back to BLAKE). Sir----

BLAKE. What?

BOONE. It's him.

BLAKE. Who's him?

BOONE. Duke, er, I mean Captain Forrest.   (BLAKE
    is distressed at this news. It shows.)

BLAKE. Hawkeye with him?

BOONE. He's alone. (BLAKE waves him on his
    way. BOONE passes DUKE.)

DUKE. Hiya, Boone.

BOONE. Captain. (BOONE EXITS DR.)

DUKE. Door's open.

BLAKE (nervously). Come in, come in.

DUKE. Look, Henry, I'll make this fast. Hawkeye
    and I are scheduled to get out of this Army in
    March. We got three months to go and that

means we should be shipped back to the States.

BLAKE. True.

DUKE. Why aren't we going? Are Hawkeye and me being punished?

BLAKE. Punished?

DUKE. I admit we're two of the biggest foul-ups as far as the manual is concerned. Is this the Army's way of getting even?

BLAKE (standing). It's ironic, Duke. But it's because you two have done such a good job. We can't afford to waste you. If you went home now you'd be of no use to anyone but yourselves. I've got to keep you here until your enlistments expire.

DUKE. You mean if we were poor doctors and did a mediocre job, you'd send us home for our last three months?

BLAKE. That's the Army for you.

DUKE. It's got a strange way of showing its appreciation for a job well done.

BLAKE. Look at it this way, Duke. Back home you and Hawkeye would have to behave like officers and gentlemen. You couldn't stand a Stateside Army hospital, not even for three months.

DUKE. I know. Too many jerks. But Hawkeye had his heart set on going home. I'm worried. I don't know how he's going to take it.

BLAKE. Don't worry. He won't flip out.

LIGHTS FADE TO BLACKNESS

ACT TWO
Scene Ten

Sound of crickets over loudspeaker. When the
TRAVELLER CURTAIN opens, and LIGHTS
COME UP, HAWKEYE is seated in a camp
chair or a large rattan one placed in "Avenue
B"--directly in front of "The Swamp." He
wears a safari helmet, bush jacket, heavy knee
socks, short pants. He looks like a Great
White Hunter, some character from Hemingway
or Somerset Maugham. A leopard skin is spread
under the chair and some stuffed animals
(optional) are placed around him. There's a
hunting rifle by his side. He is an Englishman
going mad with the oppressive heat of some
tropical jungle. Obviously, he has "flipped out."
BRIDGET is in the nurses' tent. She leaves
tent DR, comes into "Avenue B" and moves to
HAWKEYE.)

BRIDGET. Hawkeye, how much longer is this going
on? It's been two days.
HAWKEYE (British accent). I can't stand this beastly
heat. Drives men mad, sister dear.
BRIDGET. Now cut that out. I'm not your sister.
Keep this up and you're going to be a candidate
for a Section Eight discharge.

(BRIDGET EXITS DR; MARGARET ENTERS from
"Avenue C.")

MARGARET. Captain Pierce, I wonder if I might
have a word?

HAWKEYE. Certainly, my dear. Would you care for
a spot of tea? I'll have my man Radar fetch it.
(He claps his hands for service.)

MARGARET. I'm not impressed by this latest
prank any more than by any of the others. I do
think you and Captain Forrest have been treated
unfairly, having to serve out your entire enlist-
ment here. (HAWKEYE looks a bit surprised at
this.) And I happen to know you've given your
last pay supplements to help Ho-Jon become a
doctor. I admire you for that. I don't exactly
admire you as a person, but we'll let that pass.
What I'm trying to do is apologize for some of
my--"overzealous" reactions.

HAWKEYE. What did General Hammond say when
you gave him the letter?

MARGARET. I never gave him the letter. I had a
Korean driver and all he did was thank Buddha
for you and Duke, for what you were going to do
for Ho-Jon. I can't fight that kind of admiration.

HAWKEYE. Ho-Jon's education just ain't gonna be
unless we get some <u>big</u> money fast.

(BLAKE appears UR from behind nurses' tent.)

BLAKE. Where is he! What's he pulling this time!

HAWKEYE. Beat it, Houlihan, you're cramping my
act.

MARGARET. I'm trying to be friendly.

HAWKEYE. Put it in writing and mail a copy to the
Pentagon.

MARGARET (turning, exiting DL). You're hopeless.

(BLAKE is now to HAWKEYE; reacts to scene.)

BLAKE. What is this!

HAWKEYE (suave). Heat here in the jungle is beastly.

BLAKE. You've got all the Koreans down in the cold mud paddies looking for mermaids!

HAWKEYE. Sit down, Colonel. I'll have my man Radar bring tea.

BLAKE. Tea!

HAWKEYE. Cream and sugar? Or lemon?

BLAKE. Okay, two can play at this game. I don't believe you, Hawkeye. This is just another stunt to hassle me. I'm arranging for you to go to the 325th Evac first thing in the morning to be seen by the psychiatric service. They'll determine what happens next. (BLAKE starts to exit DR, turns; sarcastic.) Incidentally, Great White Hunter, how do you make a "mermaid trap"?

HAWKEYE (stiff upper lip). One makes a mermaid trap the same as one would make a lobster trap. Only bigger.

BLACKOUT

(The TRAVELLER CURTAIN closes.)

ACT TWO
Scene Eleven

LIGHTS UP. We're at the 325th Evac Headquarters, in the psychiatric wing. From offstage L comes the scream of a nurse, LT. CONNIE LIEBOWITZ. She dashes in DL with a tray in her hand. From DR, in white, comes CAPTAIN OLIVER WENDELL JONES [SPEARCHUCKER]. He carries a clipboard.)

SPEARCHUCKER. What's the matter with you, Lieutenant Liebowitz?

CONNIE. Matter? Look, Captain Jones, I'm a dietician, not a menu.

SPEARCHUCKER. Menu?

CONNIE. Some officer down from MASH tried to bite me. He's been snapping at everybody like a mad dog ever since he got in the door.

SPEARCHUCKER. Sounds like a live one.

CONNIE. He's practically frothing at the mouth.

SPEARCHUCKER. Better have a couple of M.P.'s stand close in case he gets violent.

CONNIE (exiting DL). Hunter College was never like this. (SPEARCHUCKER checks his clipboard, calls out some names.)

SPEARCHUCKER. Lewis, Major Horace Lewis?
(No response; he checks off a name, walks a

bit L.) Miller, Lieutenant Montrose Miller?
(Again, no response, another check.) Why
don't these guys wait like they're supposed to?
(Another name.) Pierce? Captain Benjamin
Franklin Pierce? (He peers down at the name.)
No, it can't be. Hawkeye? In here? (Laughs.)
This I gotta see. (All grins, he EXITS DL.)

(CURTAIN OPENS part way to reveal a desk with a
chair to the left of it. A screen to indicate some
wall blocks off our view of the compound as in
operating scene. HAWKEYE, still dressed as
the Great White Hunter, sits in the chair, legs
crossed. The psychiatrist, MAJOR RUTH
HASKELL, sits behind the desk with some
papers.)

RUTH. I have Colonel Blake's report here. Now,
son, what's all this talk about mermaids?
HAWKEYE. How should I know?
RUTH. Report says you're trying to catch one in the
mud paddies. (As if to a slow child.) Now, son,
you know as well as I that mermaids do not exist
in cold mud paddies.
HAWKEYE. Where do they exist?
RUTH. In the ocean, of course. Any madman knows
that. (Recovers.) Oh, I beg your pardon.
(Faint smile.) Mermaids require sea water, not
mud water.
HAWKEYE. What if they're mudders?
RUTH. Mudders?
HAWKEYE. Is that where you catch yours--in the
sea water?
RUTH. Catch my what?
HAWKEYE. Your mermaids, of course. What are
we talking about?
RUTH. Captain Pierce, I don't catch mermaids, you do.

HAWKEYE. I thought you said they didn't exist?

RUTH. They don't.

HAWKEYE. If they don't exist then how can I catch them?

RUTH (frowning). You're being difficult. (Forges on.) I'm here to help you. Please remember that.

HAWKEYE. I'm not a Great White Hunter, y'know?

RUTH. Oh?

HAWKEYE. You got anything you want to trade in?

RUTH. How do you mean?

HAWKEYE. I mean, you want a deal on a clean elephant? Belonged to a little ole lady in Pusan. She only rode it on Sundays.

RUTH. You're being difficult.

HAWKEYE. You hate me, admit it.

RUTH. I'm certain no one hates you, Captain.

HAWKEYE. Everybody hates me.

RUTH. Why?

HAWKEYE. Because I'm an elephant boy. That's all I ever wanted to be, but because the elephants like me so good, people all hate me.

RUTH. Hmmmmmm. Interesting case. I think I'll keep you here for observation.

HAWKEYE (worried). You mean you're not sending me back to the States?

RUTH. No. We'll keep you here in Korea. (HAWKEYE jumps up like the Wild Man of Borneo, bellows, bites RUTH on the arm. She, too, bellows and ducks under the desk for safety.)

(SPEARCHUCKER ENTERS L.)

SPEARCHUCKER. Hawkeye Pierce, you ole lobster thief! I saw your name on the list. (HAWKEYE is delighted, slaps a hand to SPEARCHUCKER'S shoulder.)

HAWKEYE. What's the world's greatest college passer
     doing here? You ought to be in the Rose Bowl.
SPEARCHUCKER. When Uncle Sam said "I Want You,"
     he meant me. (HAWKEYE guides SPEARCHUCKER
     down in front of curtain.)
HAWKEYE. Let's get out of this place. It's filled
     with strange people. Would you believe it?
     Just met a woman who wanted to buy an elephant.
     (SPEARCHUCKER and HAWKEYE laugh, EXIT DL.
     RUTH'S head appears from behind the desk. She's
     in a state of near shock.)
RUTH (hoarsely). Help----

(CURTAIN QUICKLY CLOSES. Lights do not dim.
     From off DR comes DEVINE, followed by BOONE,
     RADAR, LOUISE, NANCY. They are waving
     dollar bills.)

BOONE. I'm in for ten.
LOUISE. Same here.
RADAR. Put me down for five.
DEVINE. It has nothing to do with me.
LOUISE. It's a raffle, isn't it?
DEVINE. You might say that.
BOONE. What's that supposed to mean?
DEVINE. It only sounds like one of my schemes.
     Duke and Hawkeye are running the whole thing.
NANCY. I thought it was a football raffle.
DEVINE. Raising money for Ho-Jon's trip, that's all.
RADAR. You mean there's no prize?
DEVINE. Ho-Jon getting back to the States--that's
     the prize. The honor of the double natural is
     involved.
BOONE. Where's football come in?
DEVINE. Hawkeye has arranged a big game between
     our MASH unit and the 325th Evac in Yong-Dong-Po.
LOUISE. Their team is unbeatable.

RADAR. Never lost a game.
BOONE. And we've never won one.
DEVINE. Don't talk to me. Take it up with Duke.

(UGLY and JANICE ENTER DL, also waving bills.)

UGLY. I'm in for ten.
JANICE. What's the prize?
DEVINE. Ain't no prize, Lieutenant.
UGLY. Aren't you running a raffle? (DEVINE
    groans because no one understands.)

ACT TWO
Scene Twelve

THE CURTAIN OPENS, revealing DUKE at the right
   entrance of "The Swamp." KOREANS and
   PVT. LOPEZ are lined up. DUKE is taking
   their money. At the left entrance is WALT and
   lined up outside are FATHER MULCAHY,
   BRIDGET and others. BOONE, LOUISE and
   NANCY get in DUKE'S line, while UGLY and
   JANICE get in WALT'S.)

DUKE (yelling out). All in a good cause.
WALT (taking money). Bless you, brother. Bless
   you, sister. Thank you kindly. Etc. (As
   each contribution is handed over, the contributor
   makes his or her EXIT.)

   (An angry BLAKE strides in DR.)

BLAKE. What do you people think I'm running here?
LOPEZ. 'Tenshun! (For once, the entire contingent
   snaps to attention.)
BLAKE. This is a Mobile Ambulance Surgical
   Hospital, not a carnival. All you people get
   back to your duties immediately.
UGLY. But, sir----
BLAKE. I said everybody! That's an order.
   (BLAKE looks as if he's about to blow up.

Everyone scatters--fast. Only DUKE is left.
He leaves "The Swamp" and comes to BLAKE.)

DUKE. Now, Henry, you shouldn't have done that.

BLAKE. I'm commanding officer here. I can do
    whatever I want and I don't want raffles! And
    don't call me Henry.

DUKE. It's not a raffle.

BLAKE. What is it?

DUKE. We're going to wager all this money on our
    football team. And with the money we win we're
    going to send Ho-Jon back to the States.

BLAKE. Duke, that's the most dishonest thing I've
    ever heard. You know as well as I do our foot-
    ball team has never won a game. When it comes
    to football, we do very well at table tennis. Who
    are we playing?

DUKE. The 325th Evac.

BLAKE. General Hammond's team?

DUKE. That's right, Henry.

BLAKE. So now you want to embarrass me even
    further.

(HAWKEYE ENTERS L, now dressed in fatigues.
He carries some papers, crosses to others.)

HAWKEYE. Never have to feel embarrassed again,
    Henry. Here.

BLAKE (taking papers). What's this?

HAWKEYE. Transfer papers for Spearchucker Jones.

BLAKE. Spearchucker Jones!

HAWKEYE. Haven't heard much about him lately,
    have you?

BLAKE. Great ball player. Ran from one end of
    the field to the other and left the interference
    six feet behind.

DUKE. Hawkeye found him working in Yong-Dong-Po.

BLAKE. No.

HAWKEYE. Under his own name--Dr. Oliver
     Wendell Jones. He's a neuro-surgeon.
BLAKE. I still don't get what you're driving at.
HAWKEYE. I'm the only one who knows who he
     really is. All you have to do is convince General
     Hammond that you need another neuro-surgeon.
     Request Jones.
BLAKE (eyes bright). And we use him in the game!
DUKE. Only in the last quarter, the last few minutes,
     so they don't get suspicious and we can run up
     more bets. We'll keep him under wraps in case
     General Hammond has any spies out.
BLAKE. I've been waiting to get even with General
     Hammond for a long time. When it comes to
     football, he's a pretty conceited man. He coaches
     that team, y'know. It'll be a great team we'll
     rally. You, Duke, and Hawkeye. Trapper John,
     Ugly, and for coach----
DUKE. Who?
BLAKE. Me, of course. (HAWKEYE and DUKE
     don't like the choice.) That's an order. (He
     turns, EXITS R, delighted.) Boy, oh boy.
HAWKEYE. Best ball player in the country and he's
     gonna have Little Boy Blue for his coach!

                    BLACKOUT

          (TRAVELLER CURTAIN closes.)

ACT TWO
Scene Thirteen

In the darkness, most of the cast who would normally
   be watching the football game will move in from
   DR and DL, excluding, naturally, HAWKEYE,
   DUKE, BLAKE, TRAPPER and SPEARCHUCKER.
   Voice over the loudspeaker is dry and
   professional.)

VOICE. . . . And as football players go, Blake's
   MASH team might do okay as table tennis
   players--three minutes to play--score is
   Hammond 24, Blake 21 and how they got that 21
   is up for grabs--first-and-ten for the home
   forces on the visitors' thirty-five-yard line and
   time has been called. (Weary.) Again.

(LIGHTS SLAM UP fast and bright revealing the cast
   lined in front of the curtain, looking out into the
   audience which is the field. One has binoculars,
   another a bass drum. Some nurses have paper
   pom-poms, etc. Cast is cheering.)

ALL (cheers).
          With an M
          With an A
          With an S
          With an H

(Repeat faster and louder.)
　　　With an M
　　　With an A
　　　With an S
　　　With an H
(Repeat again, ending with:)
　　　MASHED POTATOES!

(The drum is banged, and out of breath, panting
　　　like a hound dog, TRAPPER lopes in from DR
　　　dressed in football pads and helmet.)

TRAPPER. Radar, we're in trouble. Two tackles
　　　recognized Spearchucker and we haven't even
　　　used him yet. (Communal groan.)
RADAR. What can I do, sir?
TRAPPER. See if you can monitor what General
　　　Hammond is telling his boys.
RADAR. I don't think I'm that good.
ALL *(ad lib)*.
　　　　　Try it, Radar!
　　　　　Hurry!
　　　　　You can do it!
　　　(RADAR gets down on his knees, presses his
　　　ear to the ground.)
TRAPPER. What's he saying?
RADAR. Quiet.
ALL. Sssssssh. (All tense.)
RADAR. They're going to do a double wing play--
　　　gonna come straight for Spearchucker as soon
　　　as he makes the catch. Gonna squash him with
　　　brute force.
TRAPPER. They'll figure we'll let him handle things
　　　alone. They won't figure him to pass. Good,
　　　good. Anything else?
RADAR. Defense is gonna be bunched together for
　　　more muscle.

TRAPPER. Radar, you're the greatest since
    Marconi.
VOICE (over loudspeaker). They're calling time.
    Again. (TRAPPER takes off.) Doesn't look as
    if Blake's boys will pull it off. Pretty weak now.
    Couple of fractures, broken noses here and
    there, collarbones all bruised. They just don't
    have the grit.
BRIDGET. Don't listen to that. Let's go. Let 'em
    know MASH is here! (Nurses begin a cheer.)
ALL.
            Smash 'em, MASH 'em, sis boom bah!
            Touchdown, touchdown, rah, rah, rah!
            Hit 'em in the backbone, poke 'em in the eye!
            We want a touchdown, Duke's our guy!
    (Cheers, drum is banged, etc.)
VOICE (over loudspeaker). There's the play--a
    wide, high kick to Jones at the far end. (The
    MASH people concentrate on the game, staring
    into the auditorium as the insane play is reported.)
    What's this? Hammond's boys are bunched
    together, slamming the field for all they've got
    --Jones passes--Hammond's defense turns--
    they're running hard--Walt Waldowski has the
    ball--he's slow--they'll tackle--no, wait--he's
    passing back to Jones--Hammond's boys are
    running toward Jones--Jones passes to
    Waldowski--Hammond's team is turning again--
    they're confused--(The MASH people "live"
    every minute, peppering the action with ad libs:
    "Come on, Walt!" "Come on, Jones!" etc.)
    They're running every which way--look at Jones
    run--reminds me of Spearchucker Jones--what-
    ever happened to Spearchucker Jones, I wonder--
    hey, wait a minute!--You don't think that----

ALL.

> Smash 'em, MASH 'em, sis boom bah!
> Touchdown, touchdown, rah, rah, rah!
> Hit 'em in the backbone, poke 'em in the eye!
> We want a touchdown now, Hawkeye!

(Scene is alive with noise, excitement. HO-JON,
     leaning on a crutch, his chest taped with
     bandages, hobbles in and watches the finish with
     great interest.)

VOICE (over loudspeaker). Jones is running right
     through the disorganized defense and leaving the
     tackles in the mud--look at him run--look at
     that--I don't believe it--touchdown! (Offstage
     sound of gunfire to signal game's end.)

ALL.

> Touchdown, touchdown, touchdown!
> (Excitement, cheers. A couple of the men
> hoist HO-JON up to their shoulders. CAST
> freezes in position.)

LIGHTS FADE TO BLACKNESS

ACT TWO
Scene Fourteen

Now, for the first time since the play began, the
     stage is totally quiet. A strange quiet, almost
     sad. Softly, the sound of some Oriental music
     comes over the loudspeaker, the effect rather
     plaintive. Music continues for a few seconds
     and the curtains slowly part and music fades.
     DUKE and HAWKEYE are in "The Swamp."
     They're buckling up packed duffel bags.)

DUKE. Got everything?

HAWKEYE. Yeah.

DUKE. Gonna be good to see the ole U.S.A. again.

HAWKEYE. Yeah.

DUKE. Adios, South Korea, huh, Hawkeye?

HAWKEYE. Yeah.

DUKE. That all you can say?

HAWKEYE. Yeah--y'know, in a way, I'm gonna miss
     this place. Never thought I would. Henry,
     Houlihan, Bridget, Radar, the Bonwit Sisters.
     Lots of memories.

DUKE. Don't turn mushy on me, Hawkeye. I cry
     easy.

HAWKEYE (disappointedly). Kinda thought someone
     would drop in and say good-bye.

DUKE. Come on. Let's get out of here. (They move

to the right exit of "The Swamp.")

(During this brief scene, TRAPPER, WALT and
     UGLY have ENTERED from behind the nurses'
     tent into "Avenue A." LOUISE, JANICE, NANCY
     and BRIDGET ENTER DR. From around the
     mess tent come BOONE and DEVINE. From DL
     ENTER MARGARET, HO-JON and LOPEZ.
     OTHERS can be placed as best fits the stage
     composition. Eventually, most of the company
     will be on stage. HAWKEYE and DUKE walk in
     front of "The Swamp," standing in the middle
     of "Avenue B." They survey the crowd. No
     one speaks, until:)

HAWKEYE. Guess this is it.
DUKE (waving). See ya.
BRIDGET (deeply felt). Gonna miss you boys.
HAWKEYE (meaning HO-JON). Take good care of
     him. He's got to take a long trip pretty soon.
MARGARET. He's in good hands.
HO-JON (chest out). Gonna be number one surgeon
     in Korea some day.

(BLAKE strides in DR.)

BLAKE (from DR). What is this! What's going on!
     (Sees the farewell scene, softens.) Oh, it's
     you two.
DUKE. Admit it, Henry. You're gonna miss us.
BLAKE. Me? (Pause.) Darn right I am. Surprise
     for you. (Turns R.) General.

(GENERAL HAMMOND ENTERS DR.)

LOPEZ. 'Tenshun!
HAMMOND. Ah, shut up. (Crosses to DUKE and

HAWKEYE.) I'm heading south and my jeep's
waiting. Can't think of two guys I'd rather have
riding with me.

DUKE. Quite an honor, General.

HAMMOND. Let's go. Once that jeep starts it doesn't
stop. (HAMMOND, HAWKEYE and DUKE start
off DL, the GENERAL in the lead.)

BLAKE. And you're still a couple of weirdos!
(CAST is waving their farewells.)

ALL (*ad libs*).

Take care, Duke!
See ya, Hawkeye!
Sayonara!
'Bye!
Give my regards to Broadway!
Etc.

(All at once it hits that the double natural is
going to be a lonely place without the departed
medicos.)

TRAPPER. Without those guys things just aren't
going to be the same.

UGLY. Like losing pet raccoons.

MARGARET. That bite.

(RADAR dashes in DL and heads for BLAKE.)

RADAR (holding out a letter). It's for you, Colonel
Blake. They told me to give it to you the minute
they were off the compound.

BLAKE. Who?

RADAR. Hawkeye and Duke. I mean, Captain Pierce
and Captain Forrest.

BLAKE. I know what you mean. (Grabs letter.)
Give me that. (Reads contents, pales.) What!

ALL (*ad libs*).

What's wrong, Colonel?
What does it say?

What is it?
Etc.

BLAKE (reading aloud). "Dear Henry, we know
you're going to be lonely without us, so we have
arranged for five hundred pounds of live Maine
lobster to be shipped to South Korea, C.O.D.,
in your name." (A lament.) C.O.D. (Reads
more.) "They're already unloaded and waiting
for you at Pusan Harbor. We told the dock
officials to expect you. Watch the claws. Maine
lobsters pinch. Love and kisses. Hawkeye and
Duke." (ONLOOKERS begin to laugh, watching
BLAKE'S increasing frustration. Hawkeye and
Duke live on. BLAKE is livid.) Five hundred
pounds of live Maine lobster! C.O.D.! In my
name! (Calls after the departed surgeons.)
You're still a couple of weirdos, wherever you
are! (BLAKE goes on *ad libbing* complaints
about this newest trick. Some of the cast are
laughing, others are trying not to, while still
others are waving L to the unseen jeep, which
is obviously moving far down the Korean
landscape.)

CURTAIN

THE SETTING

The simple setting depicts various areas in the compound of the 4077th Mobile Army Surgical Hospital (MASH); viz., nurses' tent, doctors' tent, and a mess tent.

The nurses' tent is stage right and it consists of three cots, each with a foot locker in front and some suggested canvas backing to the rear to indicate a tent "effect." There are two entrances into the nurses' tent: one downstage right and the other upstage right. The cots in the nurses' tent are angled so that they do not face the audience, but instead somewhat face the doctors' tent, which occupies stage center.

The doctors', or surgeons' tent, dubbed "The Swamp" with a sign tacked up somewhere to indicate such, has four cots, each with a foot locker in front and the canvas backing to emphasize the tent "effect." Between the nurses' tent and "The Swamp" there is a thoroughfare referred to as "Avenue A." Two entrances serve "The Swamp," one stage right, one left. The playing area in front of "The Swamp," which would actually be outside the tent, is referred to as "Avenue B."

The mess tent is stage left, again with a canvas "effect." The space between "The Swamp" and the mess tent is referred to as "Avenue C."

The cooking area is in the back of the mess tent. If this presents any problem, then the cooking area may be located offstage, supposedly in another section of the mess tent, out of the audience's sight and reached via a rear flap. There is a serving counter in the tent and there are two wooden tables with benches.

111

One table is downstage in the tent and the other upstage, but pulled out enough for audience sightlines. The entrance into the mess tent is upstage left, coming in from "Avenue C."

If the resources of the production can manage it, though it is not essential, it might be a good idea to somewhat elevate the tent areas; low wooden platforms, perhaps.

Each tent has an overhead light and whatever else can be added to enhance the working and battle area atmosphere is both encouraged and effective. If the director chooses, extra cots may be added.

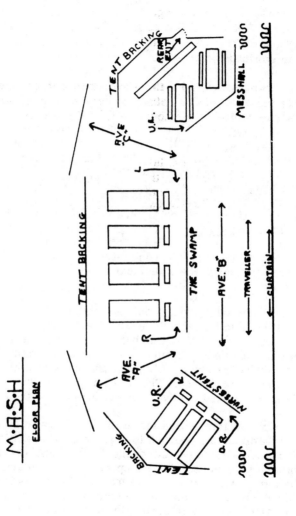

M·A·S·H
Floor Plan

PRODUCTION NOTES

STAGING:
The essential point to remember in staging M*A*S*H is that it must move. Stage action should flow with all the zest and spirit of a musical comedy.

Whenever the desks and chairs representing the offices of General Hammond and Colonel Blake are struck, it is done in full view of the audience by actors wearing fatigues, so that they, too, are part of the stage action. Before the desks and chairs are struck, the next scene has already begun. All transitions from one scene to another are done in this fashion, so the effect is of one picture blending into another. There is always something happening onstage. If the desks and chairs can be left DR and DL without detracting from other scenes /this will depend on the construction of the individual stage/, so much the better.

If the individual production can muster some sophisticated lighting, the director may wish to dim the illumination on those playing areas where the action is not of prime importance, and bring it up again when the action returns. It's by no means essential, but is worth considering. The vital point is that the action flow quickly and easily from one incident to the next.

The production called for in the text is quite simple but the director may wish to elaborate with additional Korean costumes, atmospheric lighting, creative blocking business. For example, a colorful touch can be added by having a Korean man wearing a "Syngman Rhee" costume, which is the traditional Korean garb for older men: a floor-length white tunic with a tall black hat and cane.

The traveller curtain is not meant to represent any certain locale but rather a neutral background in front of which any number of scenes can be played. If resources of the production permit, some abstract Korean or military pattern might be painted on. If a traveller curtain is not practical, then the regular stage curtain will suffice, with the performers positioned in front of it, making entrances and exits from downstage right and downstage left. The director may wish to have some entrances made from the audience if there are any serviceable side steps. A third alternative is to dispense with the curtain altogether. This works, of course, for arena staging, but for proscenium presentation it will require some stylized blocking between scene shifts and some reliance on atmospheric lighting. A traveller curtain is the best bet.

CAST:

Since there are many small parts, doubling and even tripling is possible. For example, the Bonwit Sisters of Act II may be nurses and Korean women of Act I. Congresswoman Goldfarb in Act I may be Major Ruth Haskell of Act II. Mercy Lodge and Miss Randazzle in Act II may be nurses in Act I. Captain Burns in Act I can become the sportscaster's voice in Act II. Spearchucker of Act II can portray Korean Man of Act I and so forth.

Many of the scenes require only limited rehearsal, so director will find the large cast no great problem since he or she will only be concerned with a core of about a dozen actors who will carry the burden of the rehearsals.

A local football celebrity is a natural to portray Spearchucker.

MISCELLANY:
Director may wish to have Walt in his Frankenstein
mask and outfit run right into the auditorium and up
the main aisle at the conclusion of Act I.

If the loudspeaker presents any problem it can be
easily solved by using a portable bull-horn.   As for
Hawkeye's "Infernal Machine," just about anything
goes and it's a great opportunity for some mechanically
inclined individual to create a flashing marvel.

There are various possibilities to enlarge on the awful
Bonwit performance. If, for example, one girl can
play an instrument--a violin, a banjo, a trumpet--it
would add a truly hilarious note.

GENERAL PROPERTIES:
Cots, serving counter, coffee urn, two wooden tables,
benches, desks, chairs, telephones, foot lockers,
cards, chess set, cups, metal tray, utensils, tenting,
medical equipment, plasma bottles, blankets, doctors'
smocks, masks, caps, papers, magazines, balloons,
lanterns, paper hats, leis, coffin-like box, "Infernal
Machine," green light bulb, table cloth, candles, bottled
water, dishes of food, large rattan chair, animal skin,
stuffed animals, rifle, screen. Act One Scene Four:
In Burns' foot locker: pajamas with ear plugs in pocket,
shirts, socks, etc.

PERSONAL PROPERTIES:
BLAKE: Act One Scene Twelve: Brief case with
    papers and bingo card. Act Two Scene Nine: Desk
    papers.
DUKE: Act One Scene Two: Duffel bag, orders papers.
    Act One Scene Eight: Paper scrip. Act One Scene
    Ten: Surgical mask and smock. Act One Scene

Twelve: Lantern. Act Two Scene Six: Shirt, button, needle and thread. Act Two Scene Fourteen: Duffel bag.

HAWKEYE: Act One Scene Two: Duffel bag, orders papers. Act Two Scene Twelve: Papers. Act Two Scene Fourteen: Duffel bag.

BOONE: Act One Scene Two: Clipboard. Act One Scene Eleven: Sandwich. Act Two Scenes Eleven and Twelve: Dollar bills.

LOUISE: Act One Scene Two: Helmet liner. Act Two Scenes Eleven and Twelve: Dollar bills.

HO-JON: Act One Scenes Three and Four: Linen. Act One Scene Eight: Pressed fatigues. Act One Scene Nine: Flashlight. Act One Scene Ten: Small parcel with books. Act Two Scene Thirteen: Crutch, chest bandage.

JANICE: Act One Scene Four: Handkerchief. Act Two Scene Twelve: Dollar bills.

UGLY: Act One Scene Five: Stethoscope. Act Two Scene Three: Anesthetic mask. Act Two Scene Twelve: Dollar bills.

FATHER MULCAHY: Act One Scene Two: Newspaper.

LOPEZ: Act One Scene Three: Flashlight.

KOREAN WOMAN #1: Act One Scenes Three and Nine: Flashlight. Act One Scene Eight: Broom. Act Two Scene Three: Ceremonial bell.

KOREAN WOMAN #2: Act One Scenes Three and Nine: Flashlight. Act One Scene Six: Bundle with cat carcass.

DEVINE: Act One Scene Two: Travel folder. Act One Scenes Three and Nine: Flashlight. Act One Scene Ten: Tray with food.

WALT: Act One Scene Twelve: Frankenstein monster mask.

MISS RANDAZZLE: Act Two Scene Four: Pad and pencil. Act Two Scene Nine: Pad and pencil.

CONNIE: Act Two Scene Eleven: Tray.

RUTH: Act Two Scene Eleven: Papers.

RADAR: Act One Scene Three: Flashlight. Act Two Scene Fourteen: Letter.

SPEARCHUCKER: Act Two Scene Eleven: Clipboard, pen.

CAST: Act One Scene Twelve: One of the nurses has a mirror. Act Two Scene Twelve: Dollar bills for those not already mentioned. Act Two Scene Thirteen: Some of the cast have binoculars; some of the nurses have pom-poms; one member has a drum.

COSTUMES:

Unless the text indicates otherwise, the general costuming consists of olive drab army fatigues. Surgical gowns, masks and caps where called for in the script. Listed here are "special" outfits.

BLAKE: Act One Scene One: Long Johns, with Colonel's wings, cap with earflaps, sunglasses, towel. Act One Scene Eleven: Smoking jacket.

HAMMOND: General's uniform.

NANCY: Act One Scene Eight: Civilian dress.

HAWKEYE: Act One Scene Nine: Top hat and cane. Act Two Scene Ten: Sun helmet, bush jacket, kneesocks, short pants.

DUKE: Act One Scene Nine: Top hat and cane.

CONGRESSWOMAN GOLDFARB: Act One Scene Twelve: Heavy coat.

MISS RANDAZZLE: Skirt and blouse, strand of pearls.

DEAN MERCY LODGE: Conservative dress and shoes, pince-nez glasses.

BONWIT SISTERS: Act Two Scene Five: Tap dancing costumes, combat boots. Act Two Scene Eight: Kimonos, worn over previous costumes.

RADAR: Act Two Scene Five: Heavy overcoat.

LOPEZ: Act Two Scene Five: Heavy overcoat.

DEVINE: Act Two Scene Eight: Heavy overcoat.
TRAPPER: Act Two Scene Thirteen: Football pads,
    helmet.

SOUND EFFECTS:
Artillery fire, siren, helicopters, Oriental song and
music, telephone, howling wind, crickets, gun ending
football game.

DIRECTOR'S NOTES

DIRECTOR'S NOTES

DIRECTOR'S NOTES

DIRECTOR'S NOTES